Mastering the Guitar

A COMPREHENSIVE METHOD FOR TODAY'S GUITARIST!

CLASS METHOD
Short Term Course

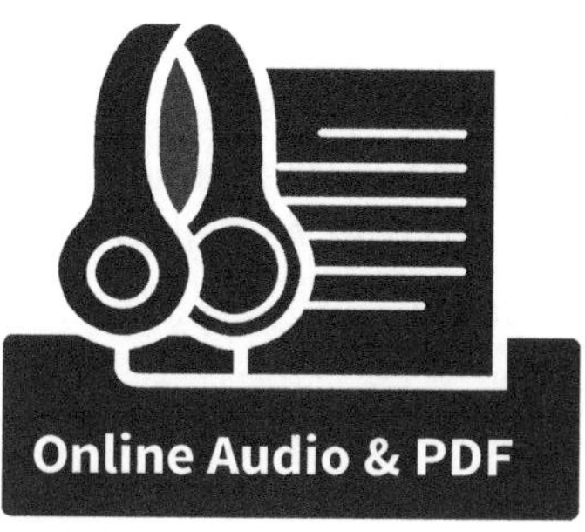

By William Bay &
Mike Christiansen

www.melbay.com/20510MEB

CD icons (DISC 1) indicate audio track numbers only. NO actual CD is included.

Contents

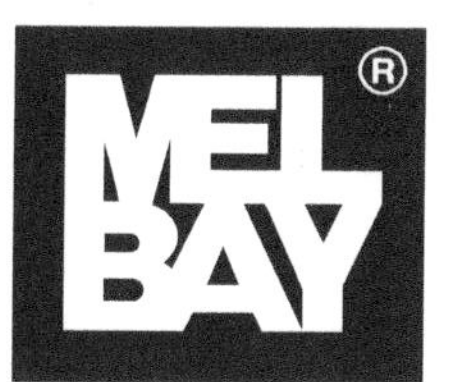

2 3 4 5 6 7 8 9 0

AUDIO CONTENTS

CD icons (DISC 1) indicate audio track numbers only. NO actual CD is included.

Types of Guitars

CLASSIC GUITAR

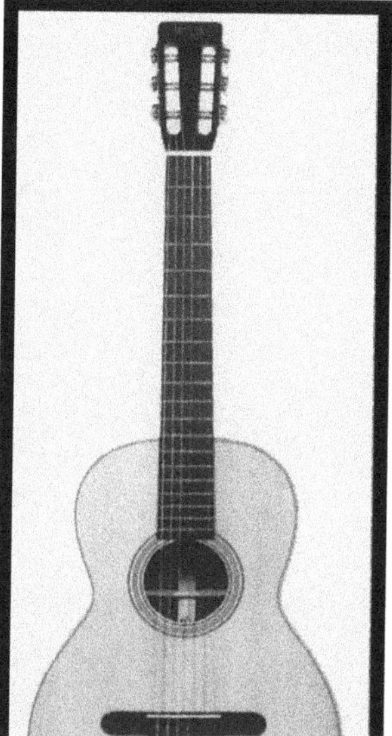

STANDARD FLATTOP GUITAR

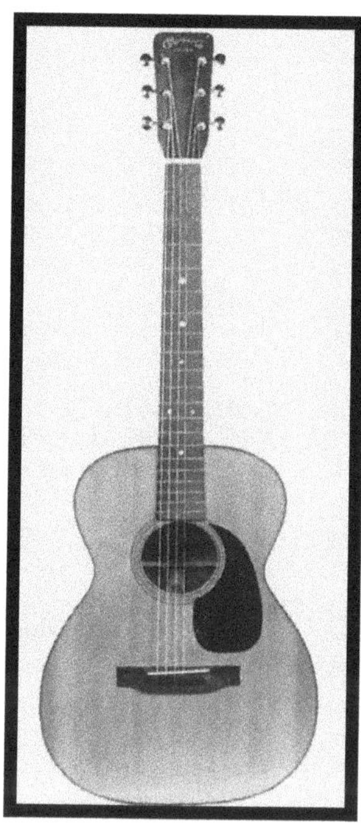

JUMBO FOLK GUITAR

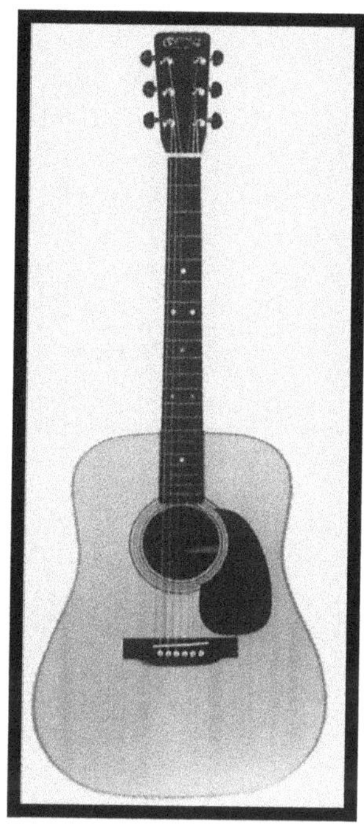

TWELVE-STRING GUITAR

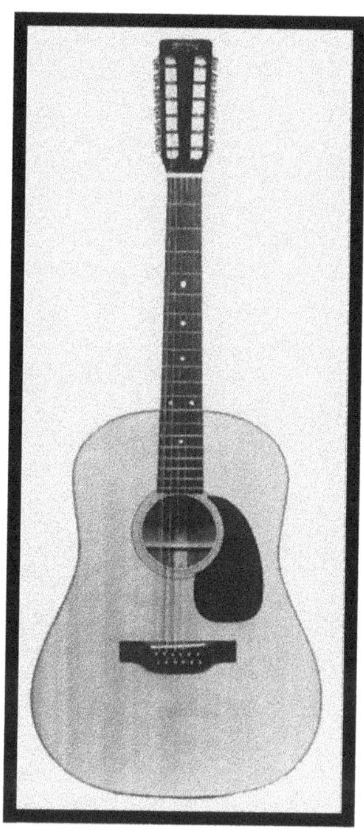

ARCH-TOP

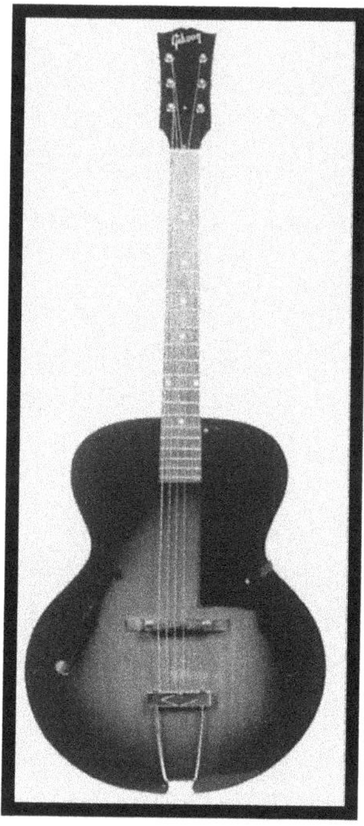

SOLID-BODY ELECTRIC

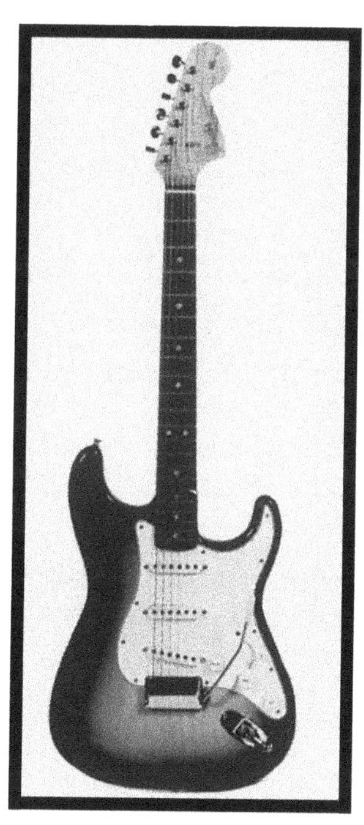

HOLLOW BODY ELECTRIC

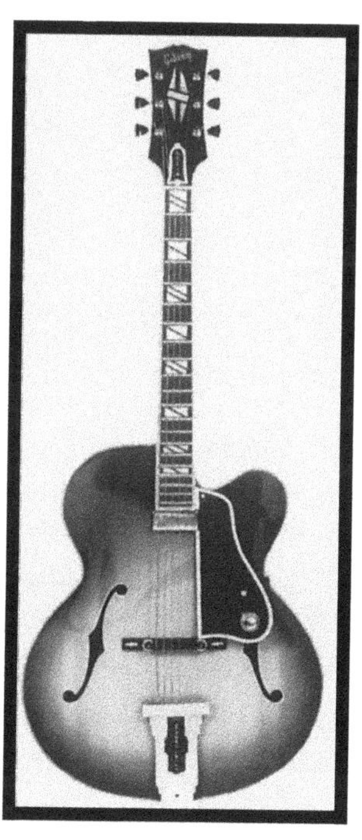

Parts of the Guitar

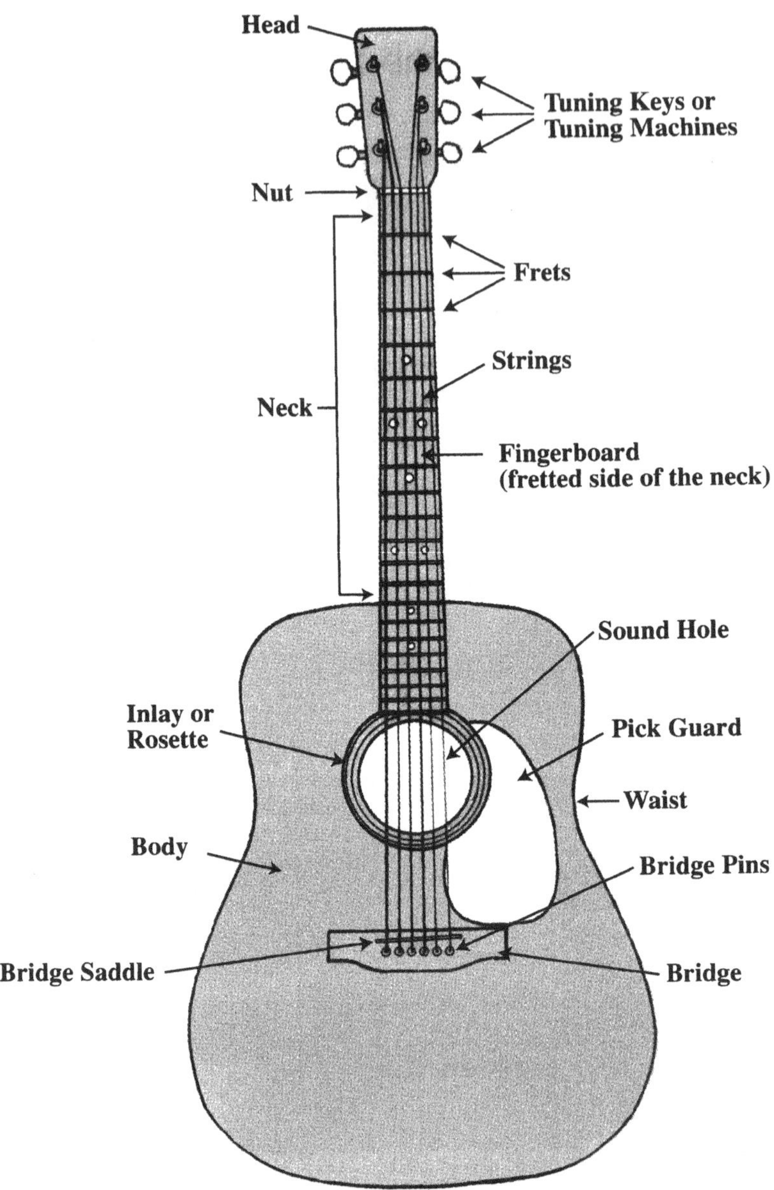

Care of the Guitar

Here are some tips to keep in mind for taking care of the guitar:

1) Make sure the correct type of strings are on the guitar. There are basically two types of strings: nylon and steel. Nylon strings are for the classical guitar and steel strings are for the steel string acoustic (folk) guitar and electric guitar (unless the electric has an "acoustic" pick-up). Steel strings which are bronze are for the steel string acoustic guitar. Bronze strings do not work well on electric guitars unless the electric has an "acoustic pick-up." Most guitars play best if strung with medium or light gauge strings. Heavy gauge strings may warp the neck on some guitars.

2) Avoid rapid temperature and/or humidity changes. A rapid change could damage the finish and the wood of the guitar. Do not leave the guitar in a car when the weather is very hot or cold, and try not to leave the guitar next to heater vents or air conditioners. If the climate is extremely dry, a guitar humidifier can be purchased and used to prevent the guitar drying and cracking.

3) Polish the guitar. Polish which is made specifically for guitars can be purchased from a music store. Besides keeping the guitar looking nice, polishing the guitar will help to protect the finish and the woods. Be careful not to polish the fingerboard.

4) If the guitar is being shipped or taken on an airplane, be sure to loosen the strings. The strings do not have to be completely loose, but loosened considerably so the tension of the strings pulling on the neck is greatly reduced.

Holding Position

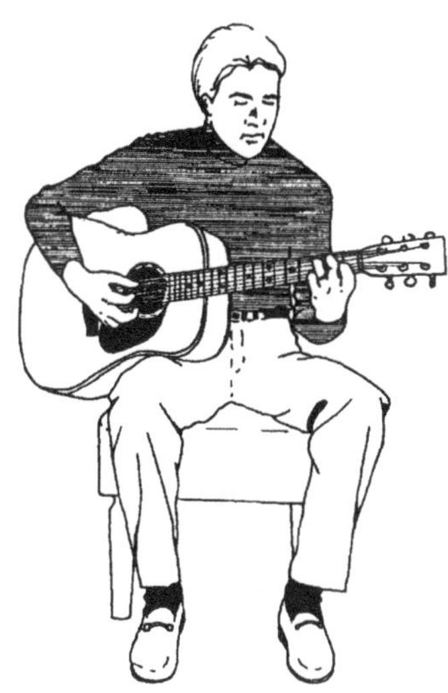
Folk or Jazz Position

If the guitar is held properly, it will feel comfortable to you. Although there are many ways to hold the guitar, there are basically two sitting positions: the folk or jazz and the classical positions. Either position may be used, but for most of the material contained in this book, the folk sitting position is recommended.

In the ***folk or jazz sitting position,*** the guitar is held with the waist of the guitar resting on the right leg. The side of the guitar sits flat on the leg with the neck extending to the left. The neck should be tilted upward slightly so the left arm *does not* rest on the left leg. Both feet should be flat on the floor, although many guitarists prefer to elevate the right leg by using a footstool. The right arm rests on the top of the guitar just beyond the elbow. The right hand should be placed over and to the back (towards the bridge) of the sound hole. Whether using a pick or the fingers, the right-hand fingers should be bent slightly. The right-hand fingers may touch the top of the guitar, but they should not be stationary. They move when stroking the strings.

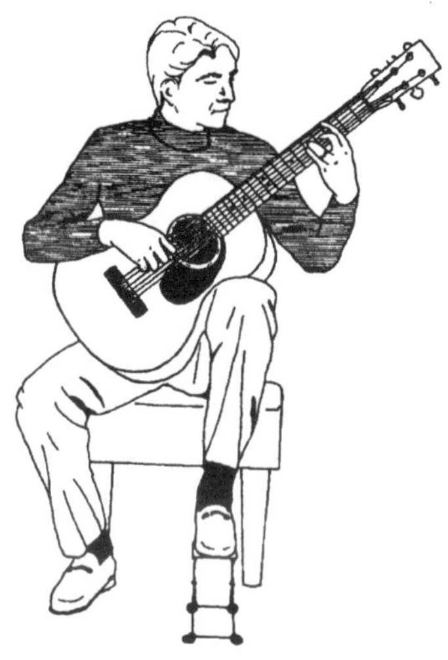
Classical Position

In the ***classical sitting position,*** the left foot is elevated (with a foot stool), and the guitar rests on the left leg. The body of the guitar also rests on the inside of the right leg. The body of the guitar should rest flat on the left leg. The neck of the guitar should be on about a 45° angle. The right arm rests on the top of the guitar just beyond the elbow. The right hand should be placed to the back (towards the bridge) of the sound hole. Lean forward slightly, touching the top/back of the guitar body. Sit so the right foot is pointing forward.

The left hand should be positioned with the thumb touching the back of the guitar neck. Do not bend the thumb forward. The thumb should be vertical, touching the neck at the knuckle. Do not position the thumb parallel with the neck. The palm of the left hand should not touch the guitar neck. The left wrist may bend *slightly,* but be careful not to exaggerate the bend.

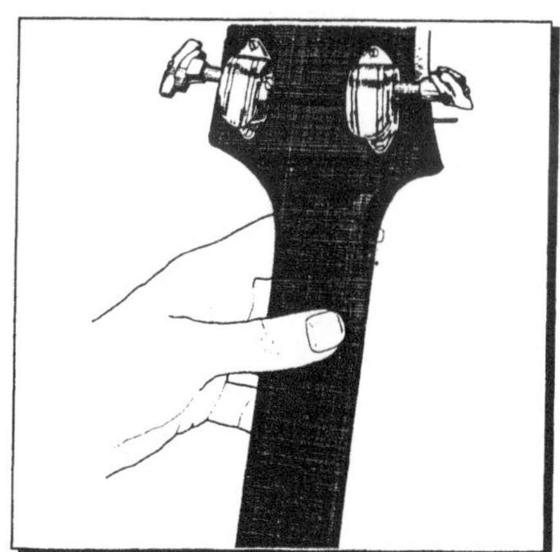
Left-Hand Thumb

When placing a left-hand finger on the string, "square" the finger and push on the string using the tip of the finger. (The fingernails must be short so the tip of the finger can be used.) The finger should be positioned just behind and touching (when possible) the fret wire. Placing the finger too low in the fret may result in a buzz, and placing the finger on top of the fret wire may cause a muted sound. The left-hand knuckles should run parallel with the guitar neck. This makes it possible to reach higher frets with the left-hand third and fourth fingers without turning the wrist. Again, be careful not to bring the left-hand thumb over the top of the guitar neck, and do not touch the guitar neck with the palm of the hand. When pushing on the string, it is as though the guitar neck and string are being pinched between the thumb and finger.

Push the string firmly enough to get a sound, but don't over push. To determine the correct amount of pressure, touch the string with the left-hand finger and gradually apply pressure. Pick the string over and over. When a clear sound occurs, that's the amount of pressure to use.

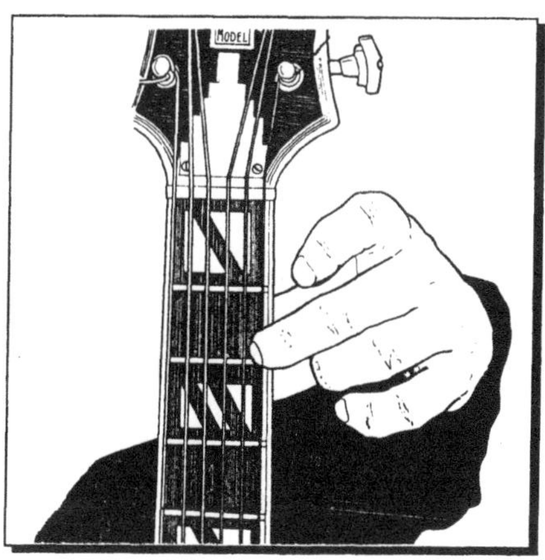

Fingering Notes

Rest your right-hand thumb on the first (the smallest) string and stroke the open string (open means no left-hand fingers are pushing on the string) downward. Make sure the right-hand wrist moves, and the arm moves slightly from the elbow. The right-hand fingers may touch the top of the guitar, but they should move when the string is played. Try to have a relaxed feeling in the right hand. Go straight down with the thumb when stroking the string. Next, with the right-hand thumb, play the second string open. When playing a string other than the first string, the thumb should go straight down and rest upon (but not play) the next smallest string. In classic guitar playing, this is called a ***rest stroke.***

Strumming refers to playing three or more strings so the strings sound simultaneously. To practice the strumming action, rest the right-hand thumb on the fourth string and strum four strings. Using a down stroke, let the right hand fall quickly across the strings so they sound at the same time. The right-hand wrist and arm move with the action.

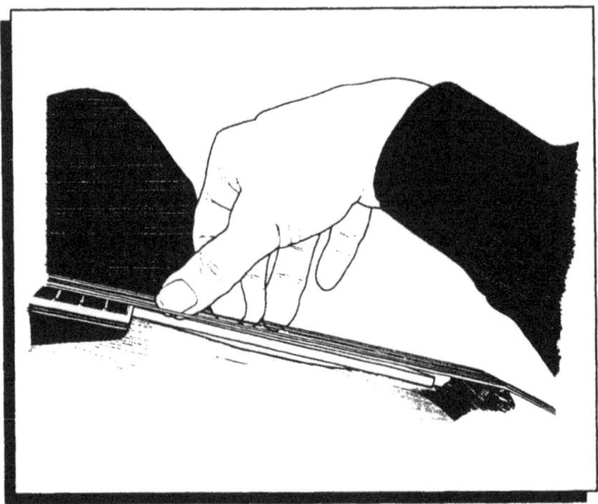

When playing fingerstyle (without a pick), the position of the right hand is very important to achieving a good sound. The right hand should be placed over the rear (towards the bridge) portion of the sound hole. The right-hand fingers should be relaxed and curled in the same manner in which they would be if you were walking. When stroking the string, the tip of the thumb and/or fingers should strike the string first, followed by the tip of the fingernail. This motion should happen quickly so it sounds as if the finger and nail are striking the string at the same time.

Avoid bending the thumb at the first knuckle (the knuckle closest to the nail). Bend the thumb from the joint closest to the palm of the hand. The first knuckle of the fingers should not bend. The movement of the fingers should be restricted to the joint closest to the palm of the right hand and the middle knuckle. When picking up with the fingers, use an up and slightly outward motion. Play one string at a time, and avoid hitting the string next to the one being played. Be careful not to pull the string away from the guitar. This will cause a "flappy, twang" sound. When picking with the thumb, go down and out slightly. Again, avoid pulling the string away from the guitar, and after striking a string, avoid hitting the string next to it.

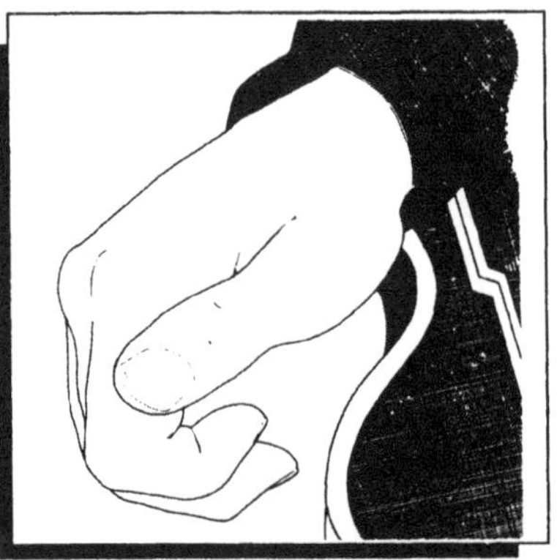

To hold the pick correctly, first, bend the right-hand index finger. The other fingers of the right hand also bend, but not as much as the index finger.

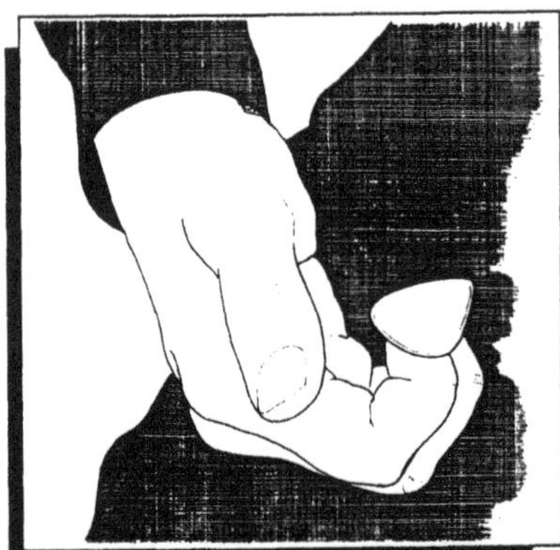

The pick is placed on the end of the index finger with the pointed part of the pick aiming away from the index finger.

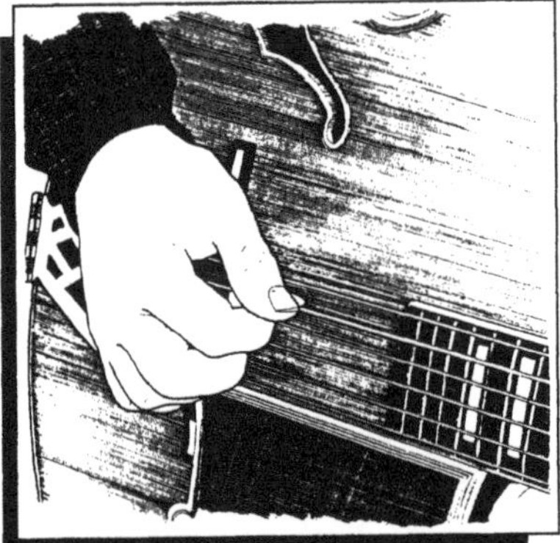

The thumb is placed over the pick, covering $^2/_3$ to $^3/_4$ of the pick.

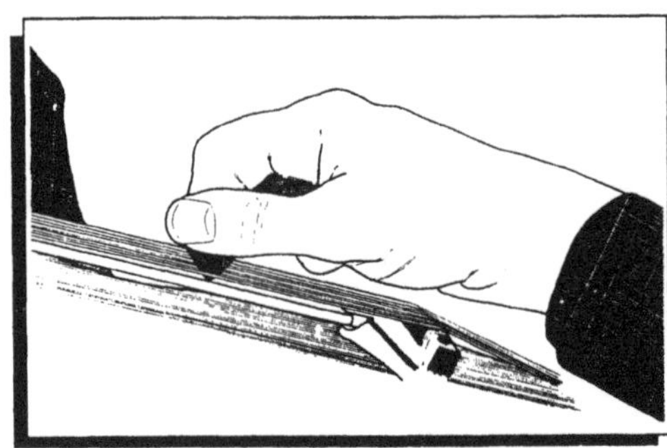

To place the right hand (with the pick) in playing position, rest the pick on the first string. The pick should be tilted upward slightly, rather than at a direct right angle to the string. The pick should stroke the string just over and to the back (towards the bridge) of the sound hole. Pick the first string down. The right-hand wrist should move slightly when the string is played, and the right arm should move slightly from the elbow. When playing strings other than the first, after stroking the string, the pick should rest on the next smallest string. This action is a type of ***rest stroke,*** which is commonly used in fingerstyle playing, and will generate a richer and fuller tone than picking with an outward motion will. Try playing each of the strings using this type of motion.

To get the feel of strumming with the pick, rest the pick on the fourth string and strum four strings down. Be sure to have a relaxed right hand. Move the wrist and arm slightly when doing the strumming. When picking a single string, or strumming, upward, the pick is tilted down slightly so the pick will glide across the strings, rather than "bite" or snag them.

Tuning

There are several methods which can be used to tune the guitar. One way to tune the guitar is to tune it to itself. You can tune the first string of the guitar to a piano, pitch pipe, tuning fork, or some other instrument, and then match the strings to each other. To do this, use the following steps:

1. Tune the first open string to an E note. (Remember, open means that no left-hand fingers are pushing on the string.) You can use a piano, pitch pipe, tuning fork, or another instrument. If you use a tuning fork, use an "E" tuning fork. Hold the fork at the bass and tap the fork on your knee, or another object, to get the fork to vibrate. Then, touch the bass of the fork near the bottom of the bridge of the guitar. The pitch which will sound is the pitch the first string should have when the string is played open.
2. After the first string is tuned, place a left-hand finger on the second string in the fifth fret. Play the first and second strings together. They should be the same pitch. If not, adjust the second string to match the first.
3. Place a finger on the third string in the fourth fret. The third string should now sound the same as the second string open. If not, adjust the third string.
4. Place a finger on the fourth string in the fifth fret. The fourth string, fifth fret should sound the same as the third string open.
5. Place a finger on the fifth string, fifth fret. This should sound the same as the fourth string open.
6. Place a finger on the sixth string, fifth fret. The sixth string, fifth fret should sound the same as the fifth string, open.

The diagram below shows where the fingers are placed to tune the guitar to itself.

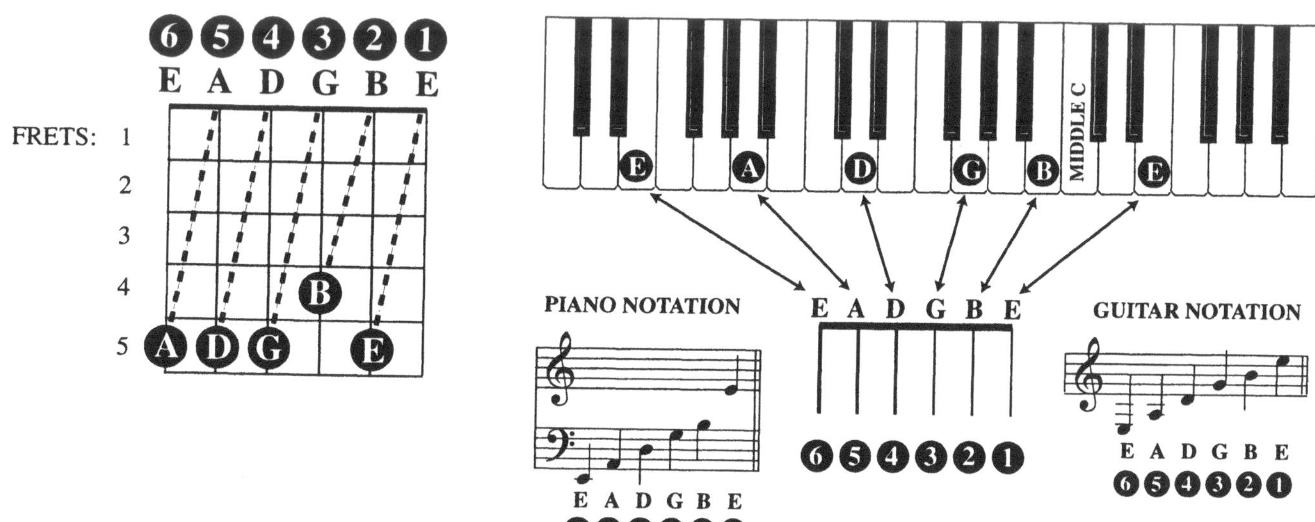

Another common method of tuning is the use of an ***electric tuner.*** Tuners utilize lights (LEDs) or Vu meters to indicate if a string is sharp or flat. Tuners have built in microphones or electric guitars can be plugged in directly. Follow the instructions provided with the tuner. If the tuner does not respond to playing a string, make sure you are playing the correct string and, if it is adjustable, the tuner is set for that particular string. Sometimes on the lower notes, the tuner won't function properly. If this happens, try playing the harmonic on the twelfth fret of the string. To do this, place a left-hand finger on the string over the twelfth fret-wire. Touch (do not push) the string very lightly. Pick the string. A note should be heard which will have a "chime" effect. This is a harmonic. It will ring longer if the left-hand finger is moved away from the string soon after it is picked. The electric tuner will most likely respond to this note.

Simple Chords

If three or more strings are played at the same time, this is called a ***chord***. Drawn on the diagram below is the simple G chord. This chord may also be referred to as G major. Major chords are those which are written with a letter name only. That is, they will not have an "m" or numbers written after the letter name. Remember, zero above a string indicates the string is to be played open, and an "X" indicates the string is not to be played. Be careful to use the correct left-hand finger. Use the right-hand thumb or a pick to strum the chords. Be sure to strum straight down using a combination of the wrist and elbow.

These two signs, (/ and ⌠), are called strum bars. They indicate the chord is to be strummed down one time. Each strum bar gets one beat. This sign, (⊓), when written above a strum bar, (⊓/), confirms that the strum is to be strummed down. Up strums will be presented later in this book.

G Chord – EZ Form

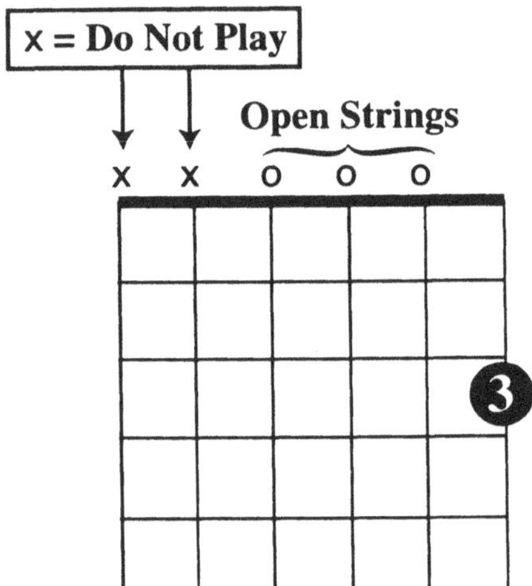

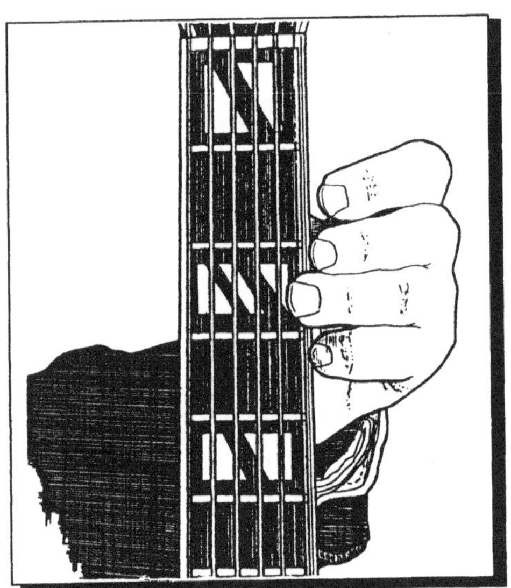

x= Do not play 6th & 5th strings
o= 4th, 3rd & 2nd strings are played open
❸= Press the 3rd finger down on the 3rd fret on the 1st string

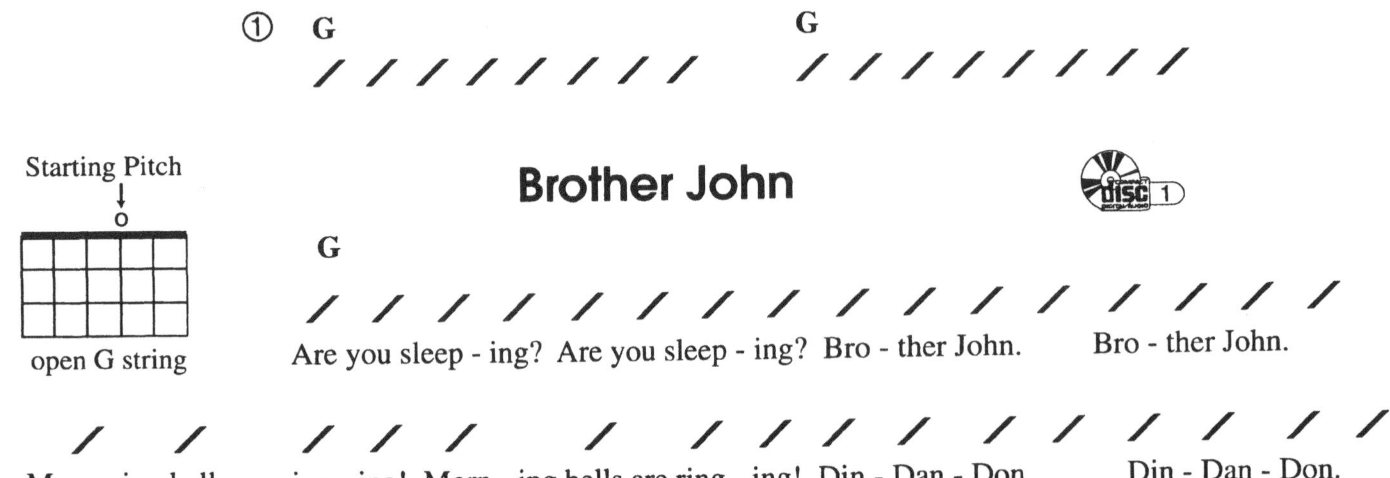

C Chord — EZ Form

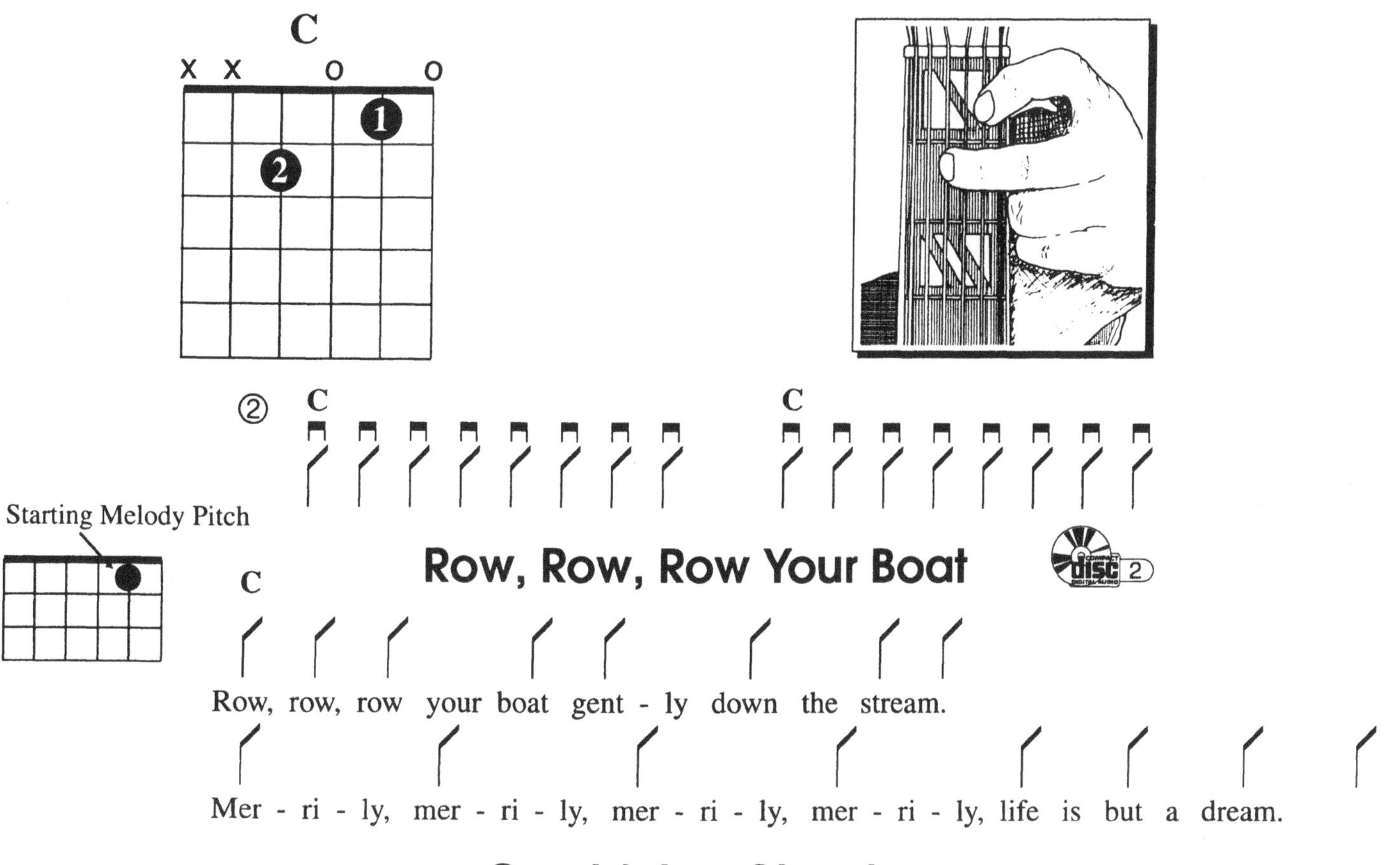

Combining Chords

The following exercise uses **G** and **C** chords. Strum each chord the number of times indicated by the strum bars.

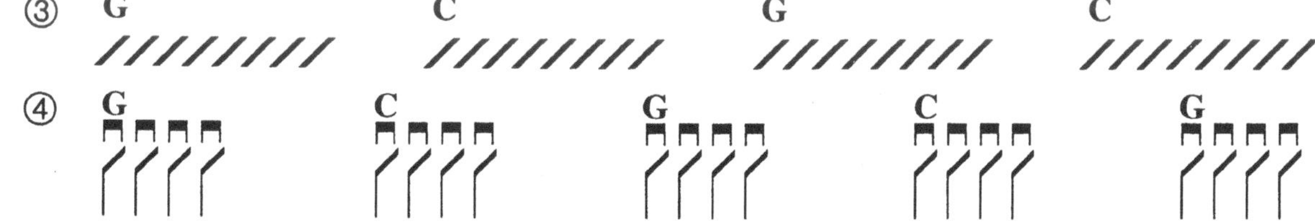

Practice changing from one chord to the next. A technique which will help change chords quickly is to keep the right hand going when changing chords. At first, just play open strings between the chord changes because it will be difficult to change quickly.

But, eventually, the left hand will catch up to the right. Then, the "open-string fill" will go away because the chords will change quickly.

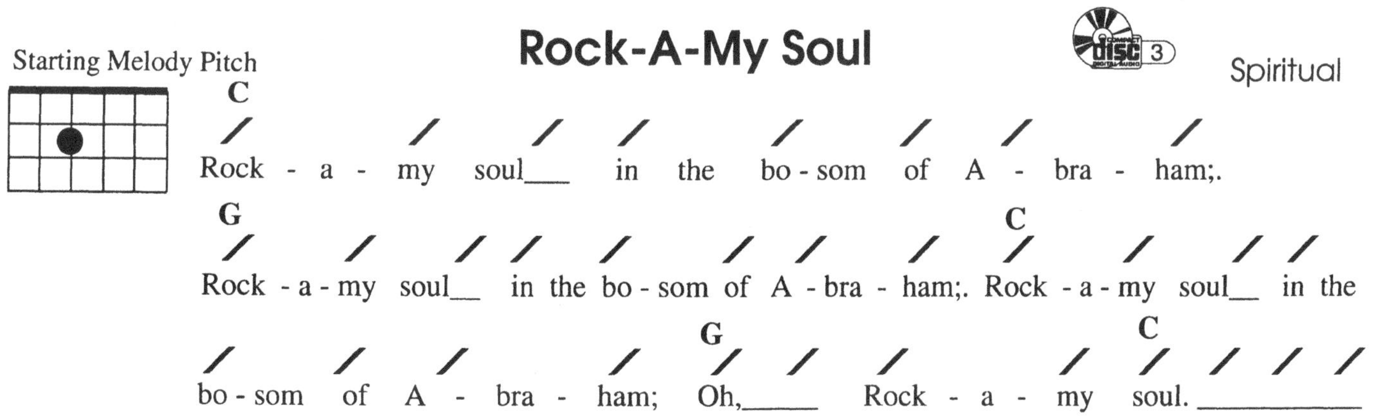

G7 Chord - EZ Form

The next chord to learn is simple **G7**.

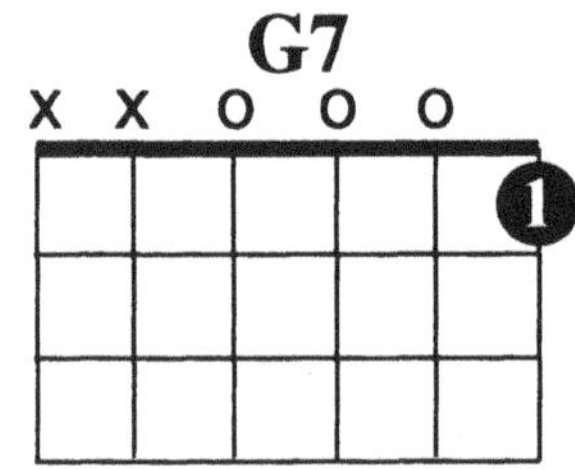

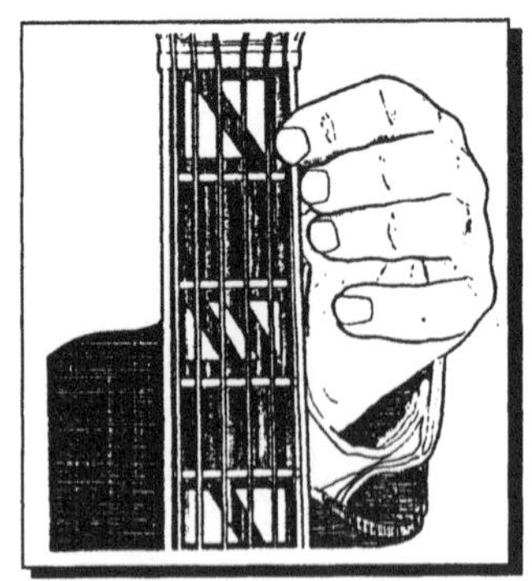

Play the following exercise which contains simple G7.

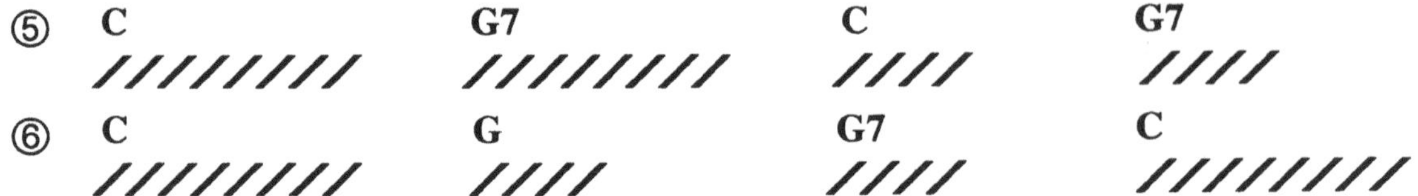

Playing Chords to Measured Music

Remember, if a song is in 4/4 time, there are four counts in each measure. In 3/4 time, there are three counts in each measure. For 4/4 time, the simplest strum is to play down four times in each measure, This accompaniment, though simple, will work for many songs.

Play the following exercise strumming down four times in each measure. If a chord name is not written above a measure, continue playing the last written chord through that measure.

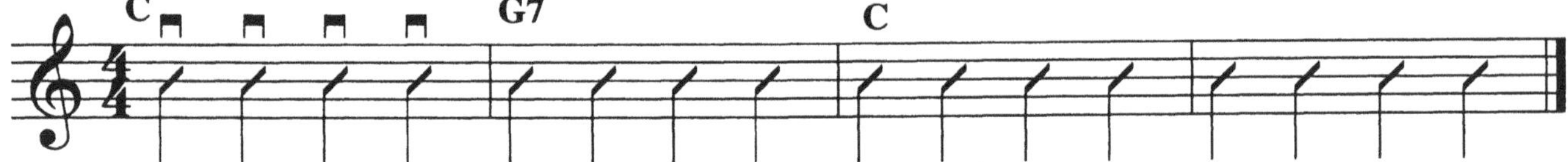

Because the next exercise is in 3/4, strum down three times in each measure.

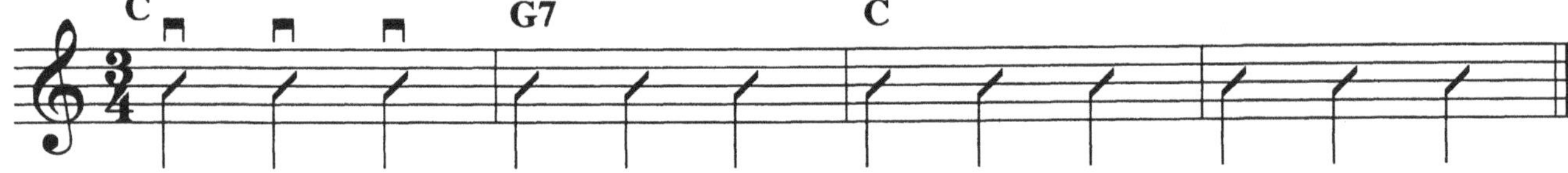

Practice playing the following song which is in 4/4. Strum down four times in each measure. When playing the chords to a song from music like this, do not be concerned with the notes. Only be concerned with the chord names, the number of measures each chord gets, and the number of beats in each measure,

Marianne

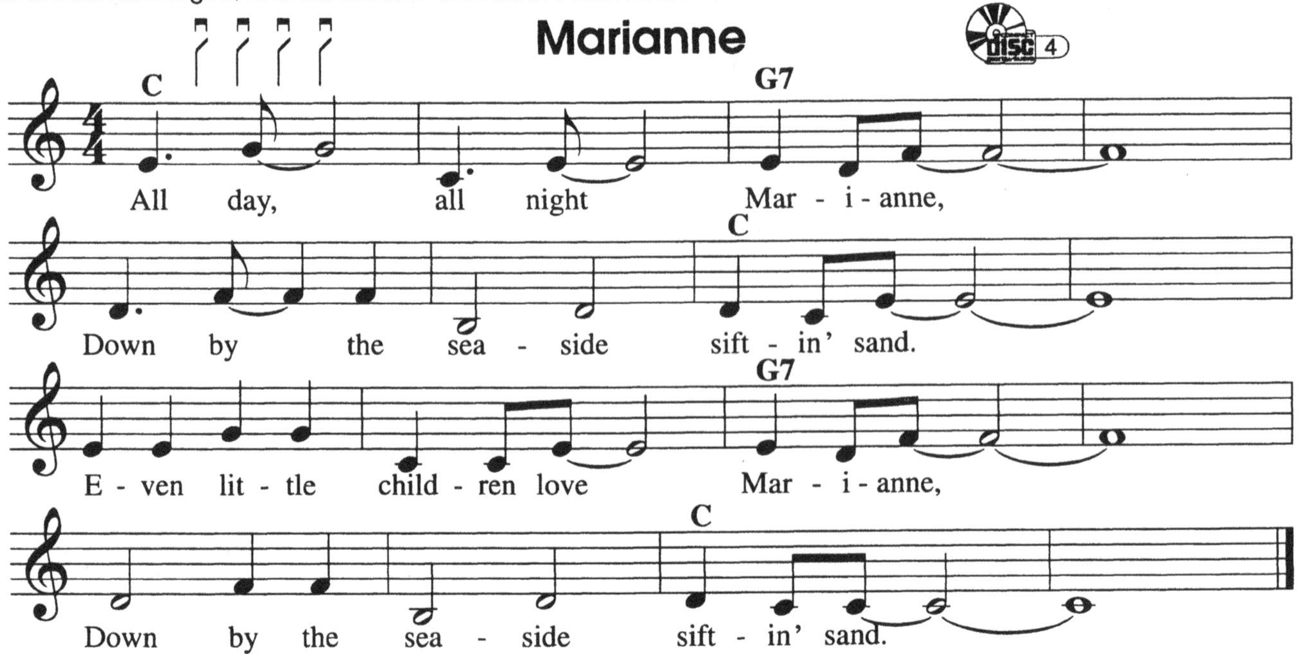

Learning to Read Tablature

Tablature is a way of writing guitar music which tells you where to find notes. In tablature:

Lines = Strings
Numbers = Frets

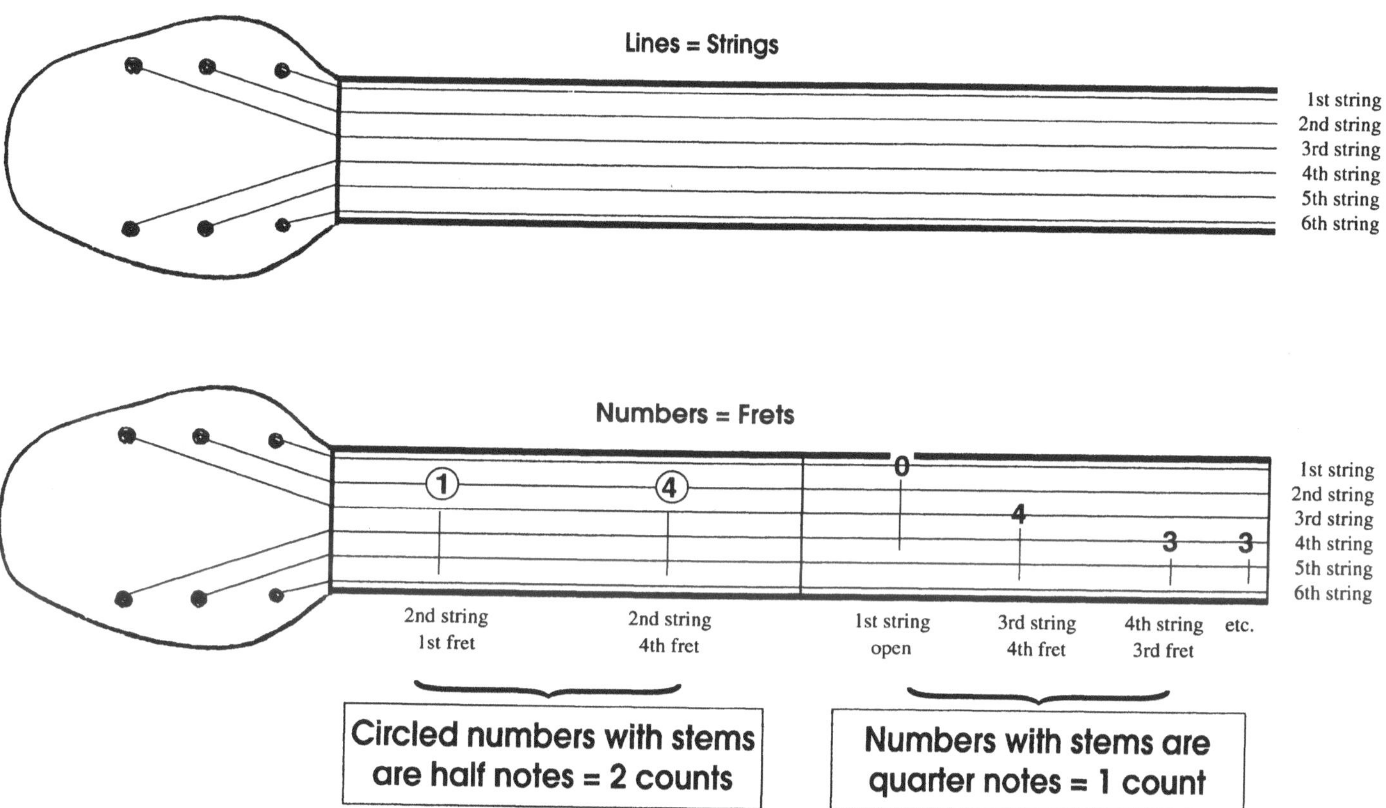

Playing Several Notes at Once

When numbers appear right above one another, more than one string is played at the same time.

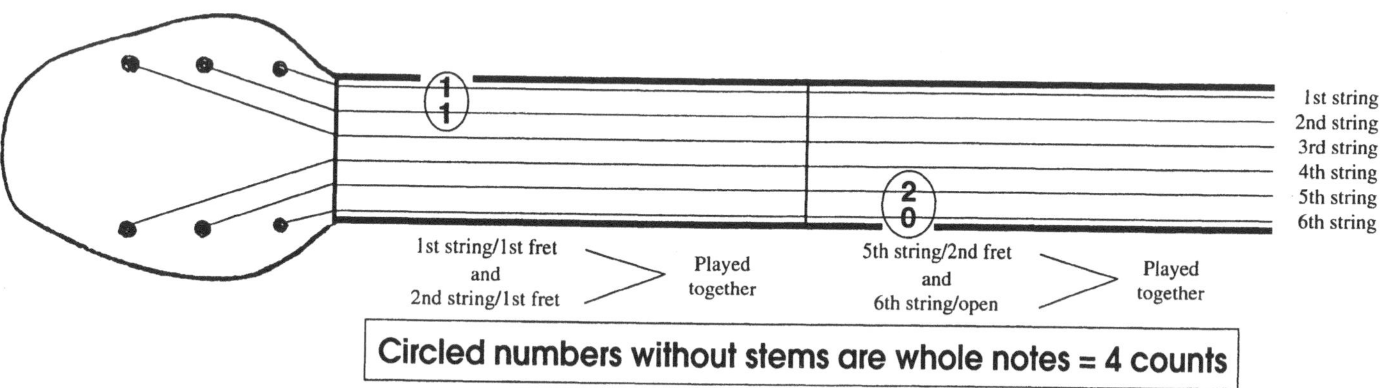

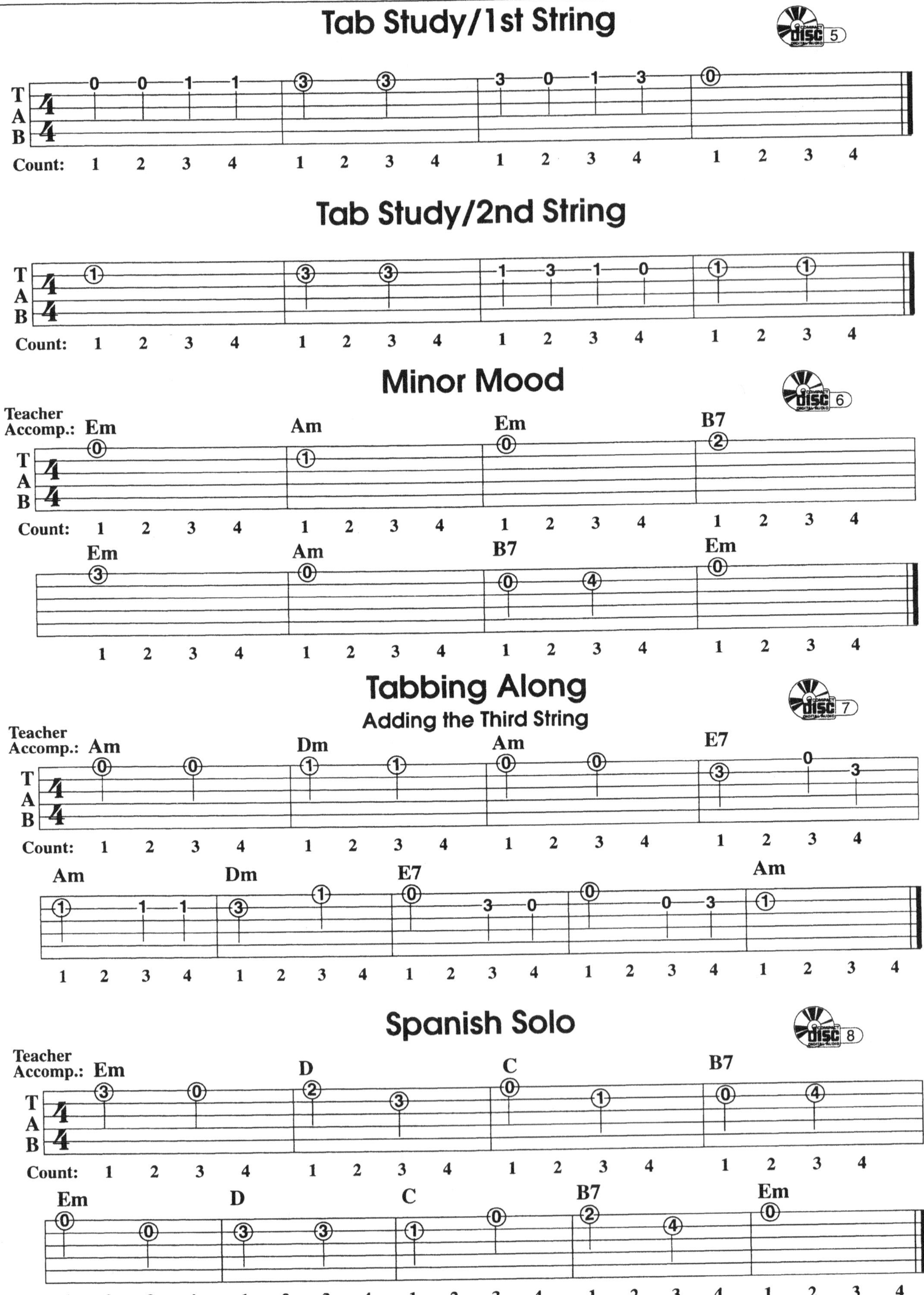
Tab Study/1st String
TAB
Count:
Tab Study/2nd String
TAB
Count:
Minor Mood
Teacher Accomp.: Em Am Em B7
Count:
Em Am B7 Em
Tabbing Along
Adding the Third String
Teacher Accomp.: Am Dm Am E7
Count:
Am Dm E7 Am
Spanish Solo
Teacher Accomp.: Em D C B7
Count:
Em D C B7 Em

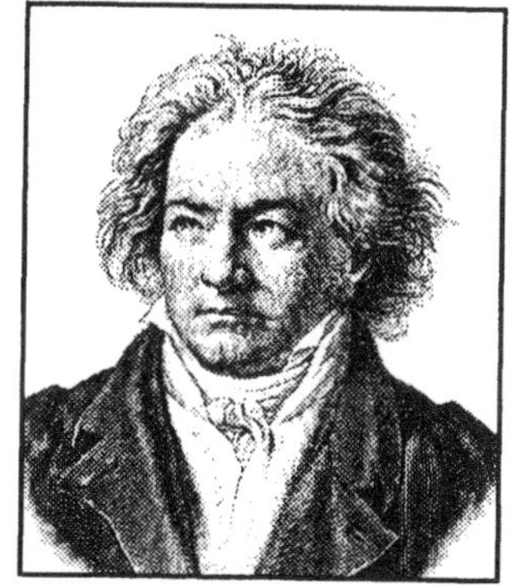

Ludwig Van Beethoven (1772-1827)

GERMANY

Beethoven was one of the world's greatest composers. He was born in Germany in the city of Bonn. Beethoven showed early ability in music, especially the ability to improvise or make up musical themes spontaneously. When Beethoven was approximately 30 years old, he began noticing he was losing his hearing. One of the amazing features about Beethoven was that he continued to compose some of his greatest works while he was deaf. His greatest works are his Nine Symphonies and they are known for the artistic development of the themes and the emotional power conveyed in the music. "Song of Joy" is a theme from his Ninth Symphony.

Song of Joy

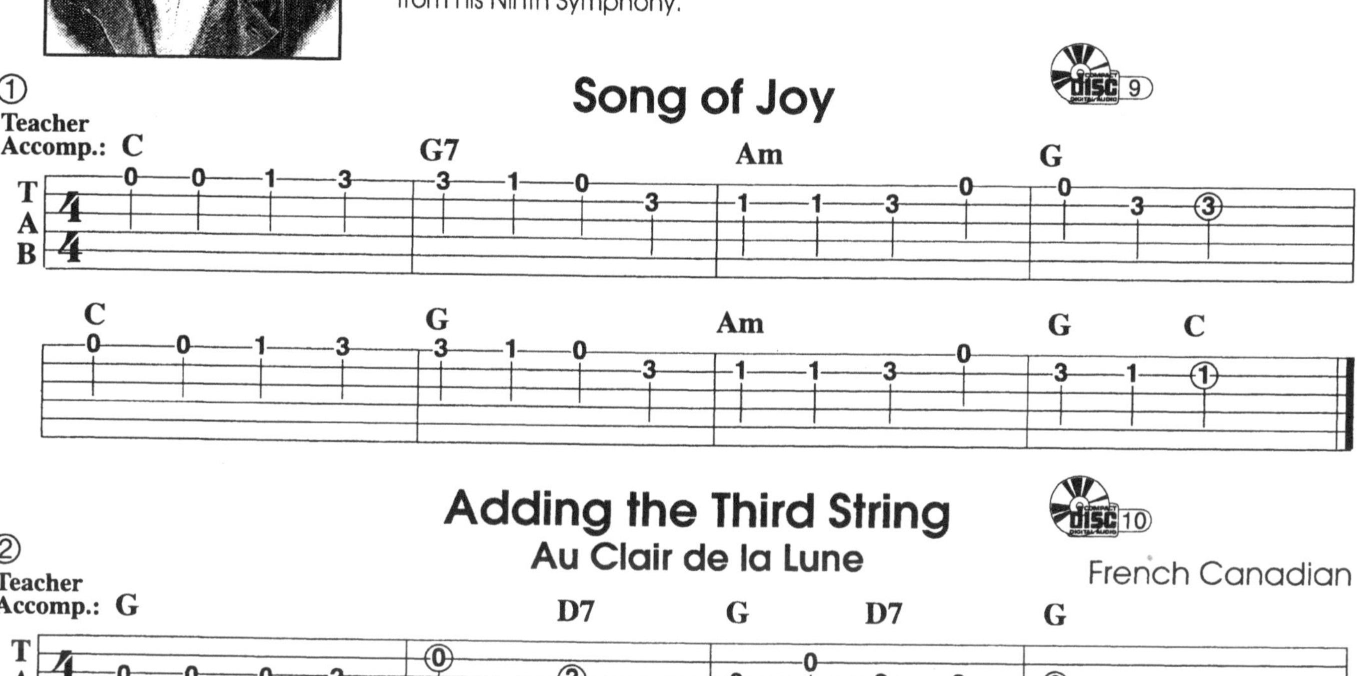

Adding the Third String

Au Clair de la Lune

French Canadian

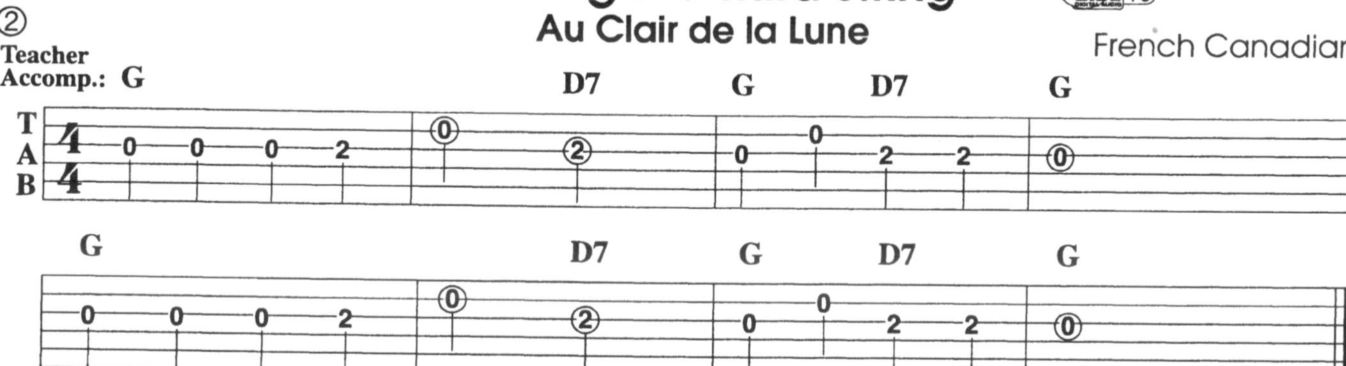

Tab Quiz

① Which line is the first string? Which is the 6th string?

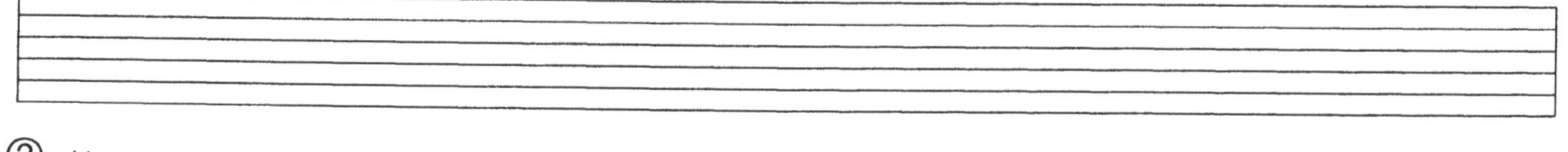

② How many counts do the following notes receive?

③ Write the following notes in tablature

1	2	3	4
2nd string 1st fret 4 counts	1st string 3rd fret 1 count	2nd string 2nd fret 2 counts	3rd string open 1 count

Guitar Ensemble in Tablature

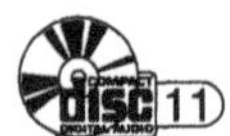

Guitaround

Have the entire class play this round in unison. Then, divide the class in half. Play it again with one half starting at number ① and the other half starting at number ① when the first half reaches number ②.

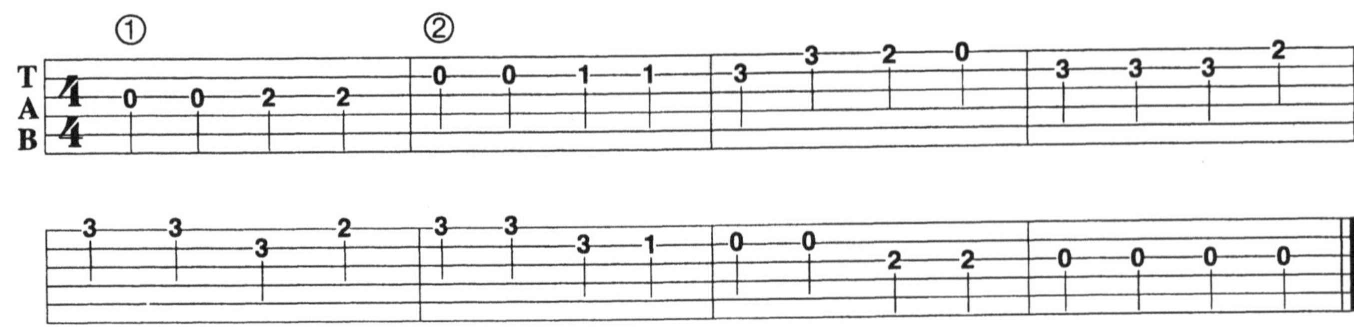

Tab Trio

The following piece is written for three guitars. Divide the class into three sections. Have each section play a part.

Where the Red Fern Grows

Suggested reading: *Where the Red Fern Grows* by Wilson Rawls

GTR I
GTR II
GTR III

[6] *

* This is a rehearsal que. In this case, the [6] indicates measure six.

Reading Standard Notation

The Staff

Music is written on a ***staff*** consisting of ***five lines*** and ***four spaces.*** The lines and spaces are numbered upward as shown.

5TH LINE
4TH LINE — 4TH SPACE
3RD LINE — 3RD SPACE
2ND LINE — 2ND SPACE
1ST LINE — 1ST SPACE

The lines and spaces are named after letters of the alphabet.

The ***lines*** are named as follows:

5 F
4 D
3 B
2 G
1 E

The letters can easily be remembered by the sentence – **E**very **G**ood **B**oy **D**oes **F**ine

The letter-names of the ***spaces*** are:

4 E
3 C
2 A
1 F

They spell the word **F-A-C-E.**

The musical alphabet has seven letters – **A B C D E F G.**

The ***staff*** is divided into measures by vertical lines called ***bars.***

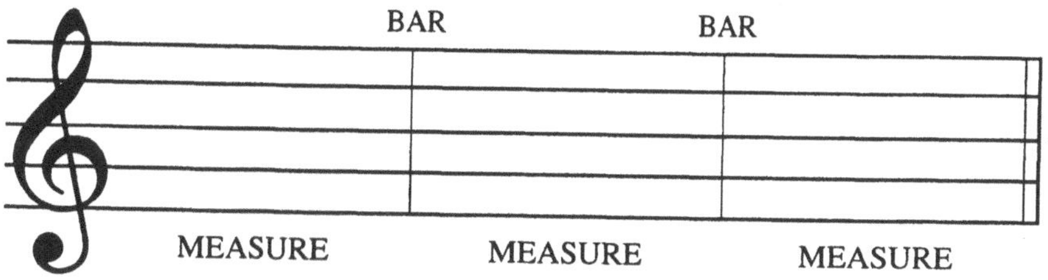

BAR BAR

MEASURE MEASURE MEASURE

DOUBLE BARS MARK THE END OF A SECTION OR STRAIN OF MUSIC.

The Clef

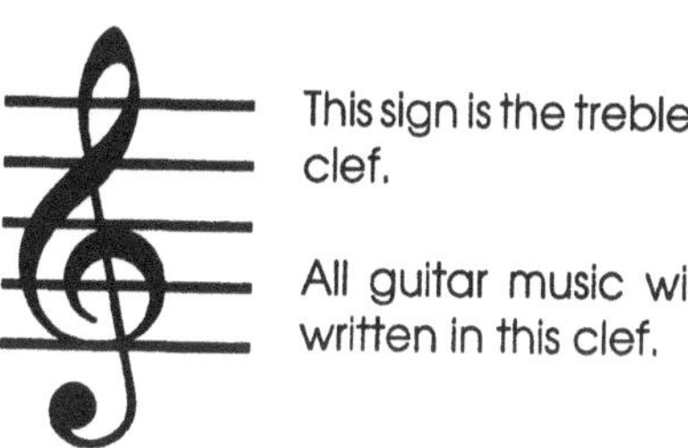

This sign is the treble or G clef.

All guitar music will be written in this clef.

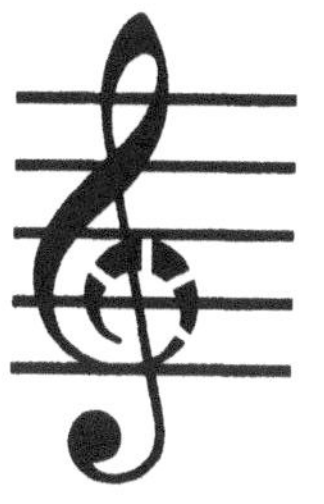

The second line of the treble clef is known as the G line. Many people call the treble clef the G clef because it circles around the G line.

Notes

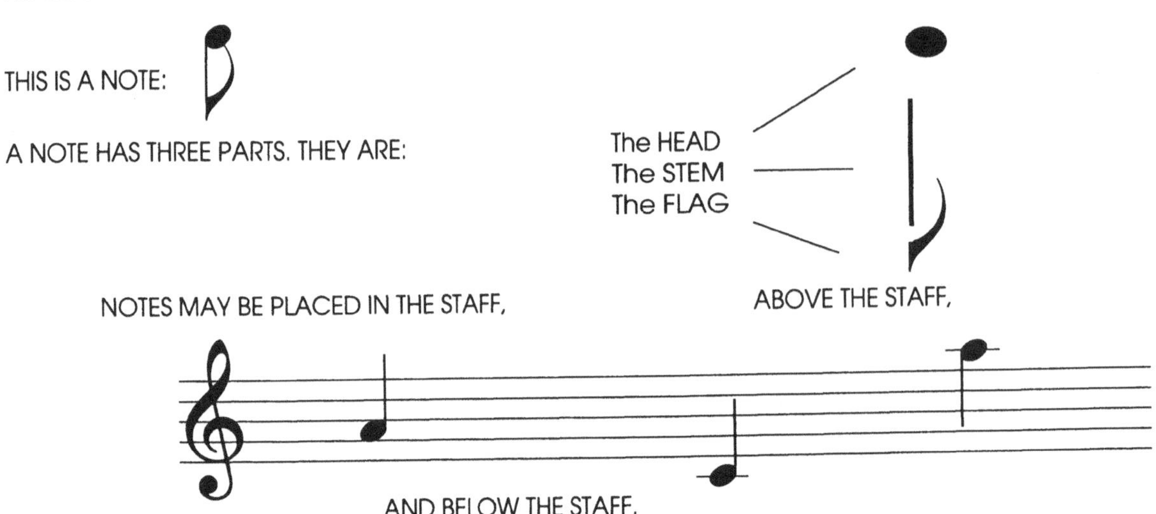

A note will bear the name of the line or space it occupies on the staff.
The location of a note in, above, or below the staff will indicate the pitch.

PITCH: the height or depth of a tone.
TONE: a musical sound.

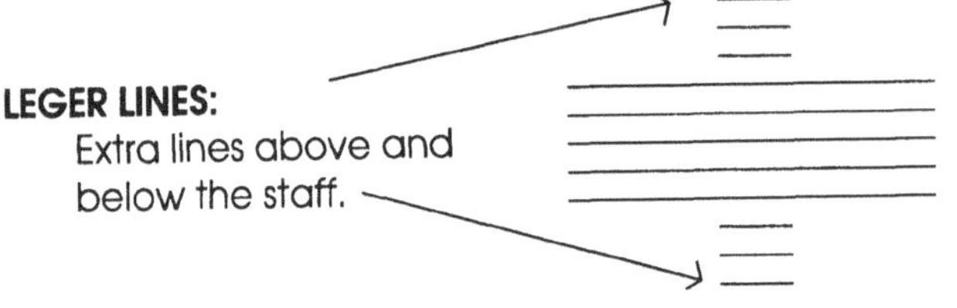

LEGER LINES:
Extra lines above and below the staff.

Types of Notes

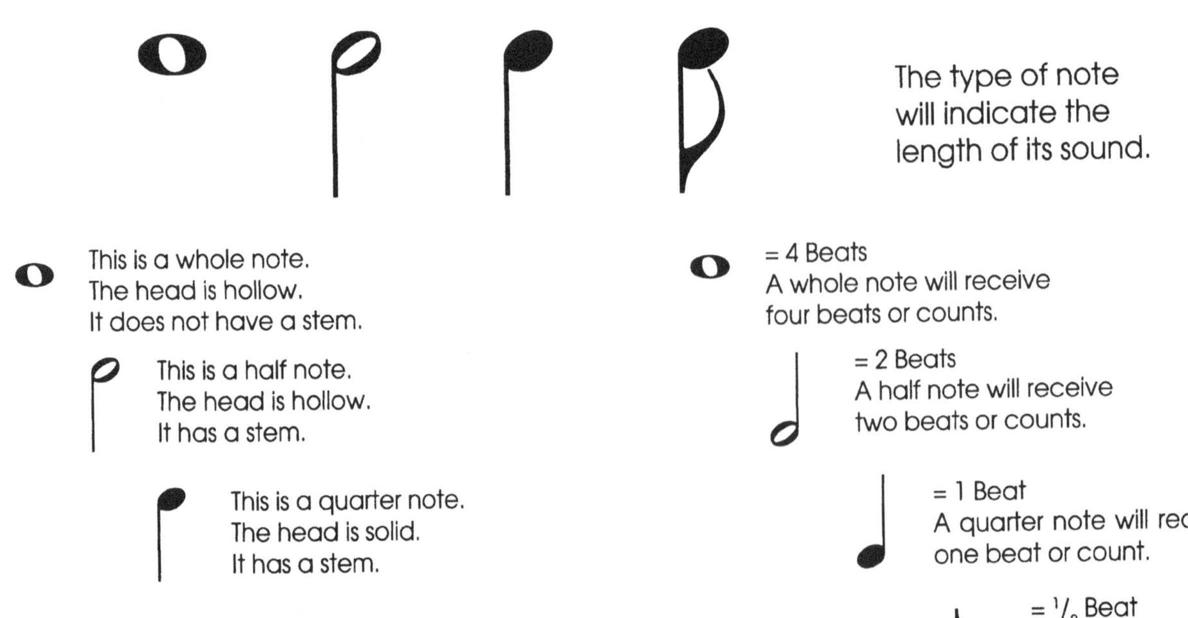

The type of note will indicate the length of its sound.

This is a whole note.
The head is hollow.
It does not have a stem.

This is a half note.
The head is hollow.
It has a stem.

This is a quarter note.
The head is solid.
It has a stem.

This is an eighth note.
The head is solid.
It has a stem and a flag.

= 4 Beats
A whole note will receive four beats or counts.

= 2 Beats
A half note will receive two beats or counts.

= 1 Beat
A quarter note will receive one beat or count.

= $^1/_2$ Beat
An eighth note will receive one-half beat or count.
(2 for 1 beat)

Rests

A ***rest*** is a sign used to designate a period of silence. This period of silence will be of the same duration of time as the note to which it corresponds.

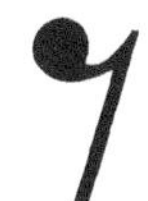

This is an eighth rest.

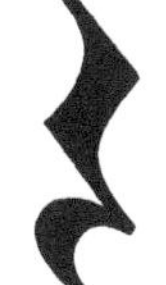

This is a quarter rest.

Half rest.
(Half rests lie on the line.)

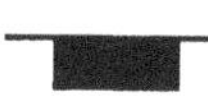

Whole rest.
(Whole rests hang down from the line.)

Notes

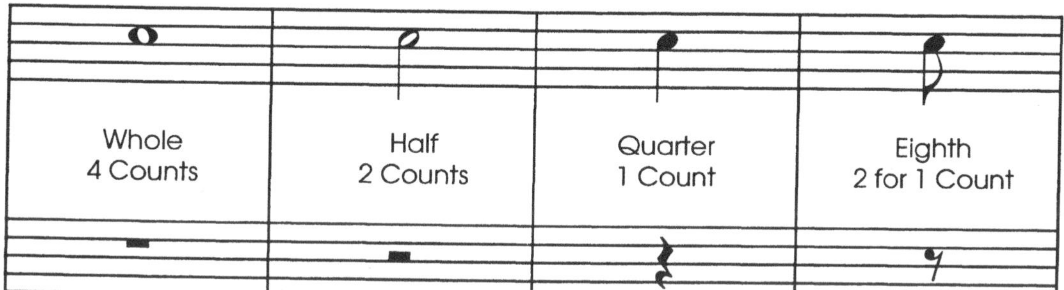

Rests

The Time Signature

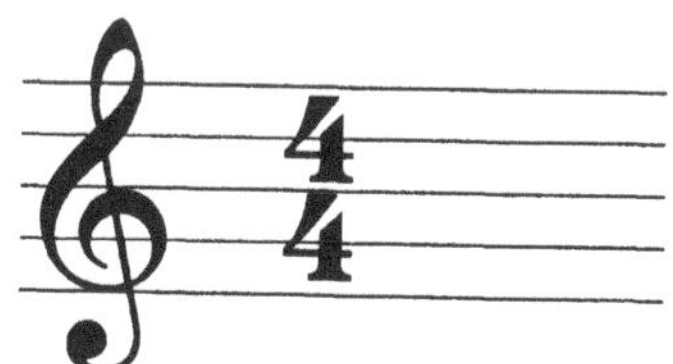

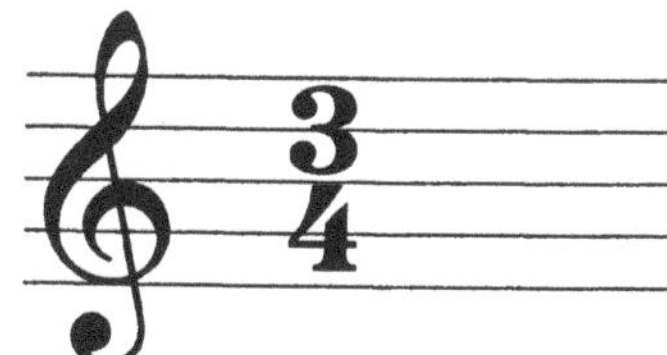

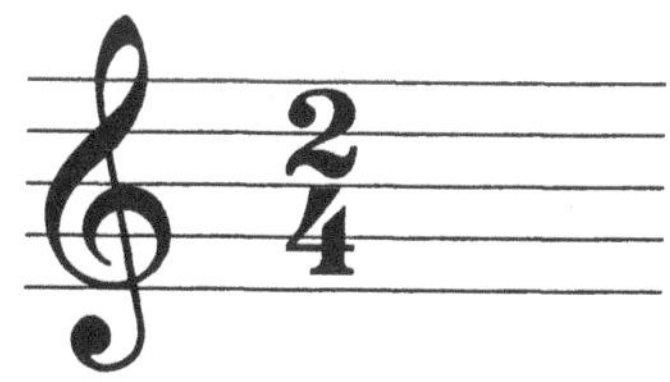

The above examples are the common types of time signatures to be used in this book.

The number of beats per measure.	4	Four beats per measure
The type of note receiving one beat.	4	A quarter note receives one beat.

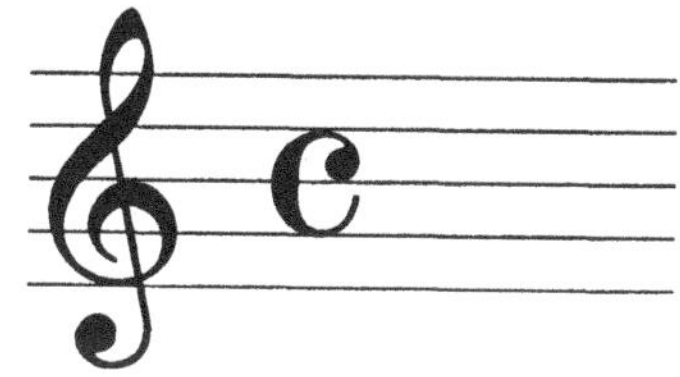

Signifies so-called ***common time*** and is simply another way of designating 4/4 time.

Music and Math Quiz

Grade ________

a. Write how many beats the notes or rests would receive.

𝅝 = ______ Beats

𝅗𝅥 = ______ Beats

♩ = ______ Beats

♪ = ______ Beats

𝄻 = ______ Beats

𝄽 = ______ Beats

𝄼 = ______ Beats

𝄾 = ______ Beats

b. Write the answer to the following addition problems.

1. 𝅗𝅥 + 𝅗𝅥 =
2. ♩ + ♩ + 𝅗𝅥 =
3. 𝅝 + 𝅗𝅥 =
4. 𝅝 + 𝅝 =
5. ♩ + 𝅝 + 𝅗𝅥 =
6. 𝅝 + ♩ =
7. 𝅗𝅥 + 𝅗𝅥 + ♩ =
8. ♩ + 𝅝 =
9. 𝅗𝅥 + ♩ + 𝅗𝅥 =
10. 𝅝 + 𝅗𝅥 + ♩ =
11. 𝅗𝅥 + 𝅗𝅥 + 𝄻 =
12. ♪ + ♪ =
13. 𝅗𝅥 + 𝄻 =
14. 𝅝 + 𝄽 =
15. 𝄾 + 𝄾 + 𝄽 =
16. 𝄻 + 𝅗𝅥 =
17. 𝄾 + 𝄾 + 𝄾 + 𝄻 =
18. 𝅗𝅥 + 𝅝 + ♩ + 𝄽 + 𝄻 =

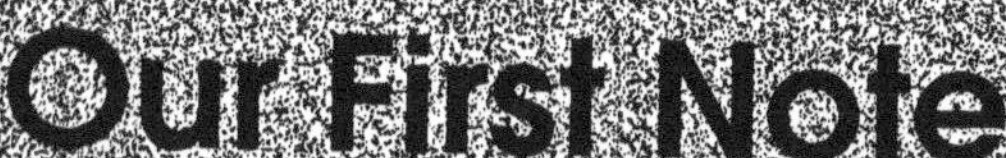

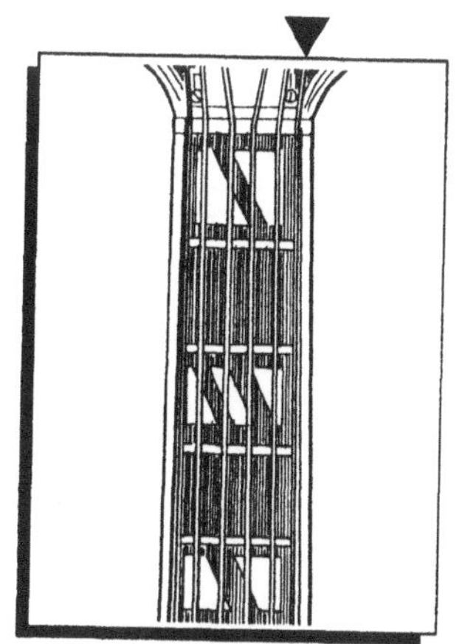

E

The first string on the guitar is called the high E String. **Our first note is E-open 1st string.**

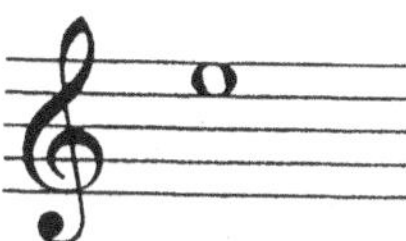

(Open)
Unless otherwise indicated, use a pick to play the exercises and solos in this book. Use a downstroke to play quarter, half, and whole notes.

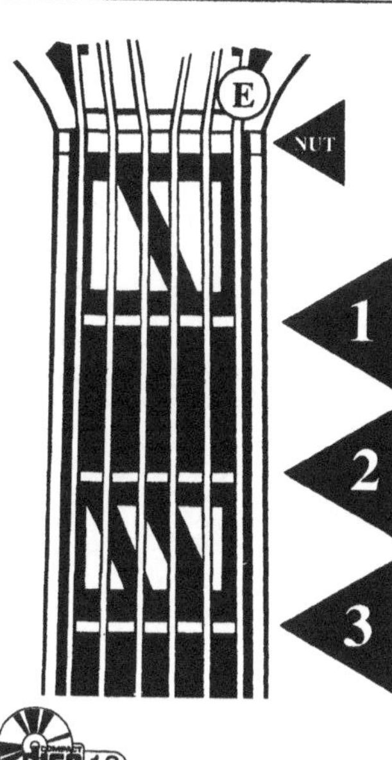

E Study #1

(Use a pick to play the following studies)

13

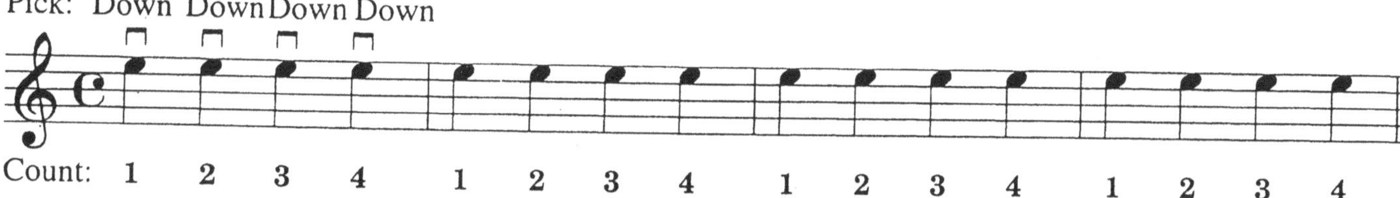

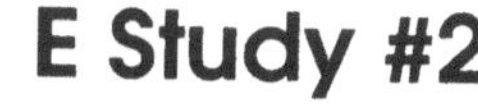

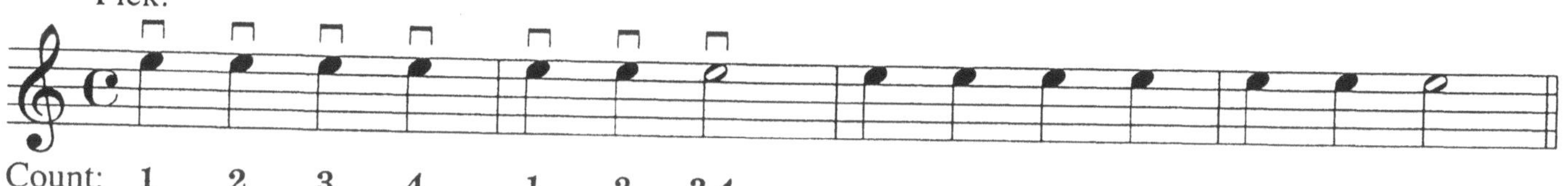

E Study #3

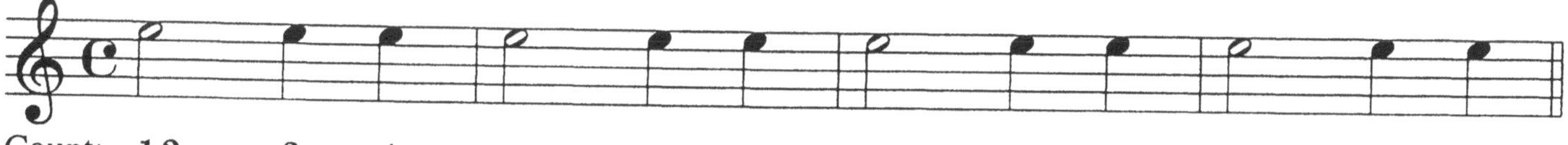

E Study #4

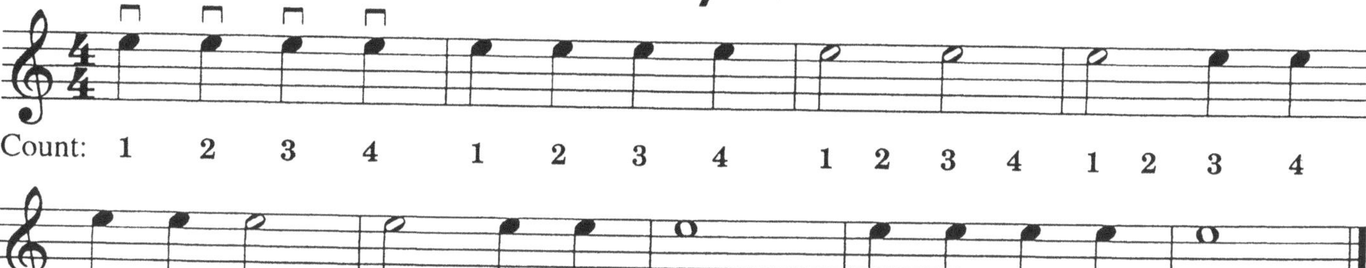

E Study #5

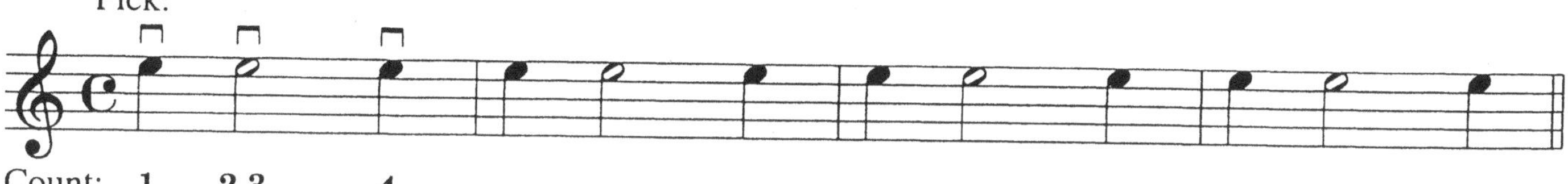

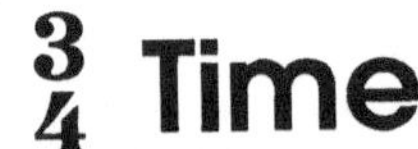

3/4 Time

In 3/4 time we have three beats per measure.

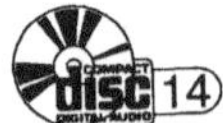

E in 3/4 Time

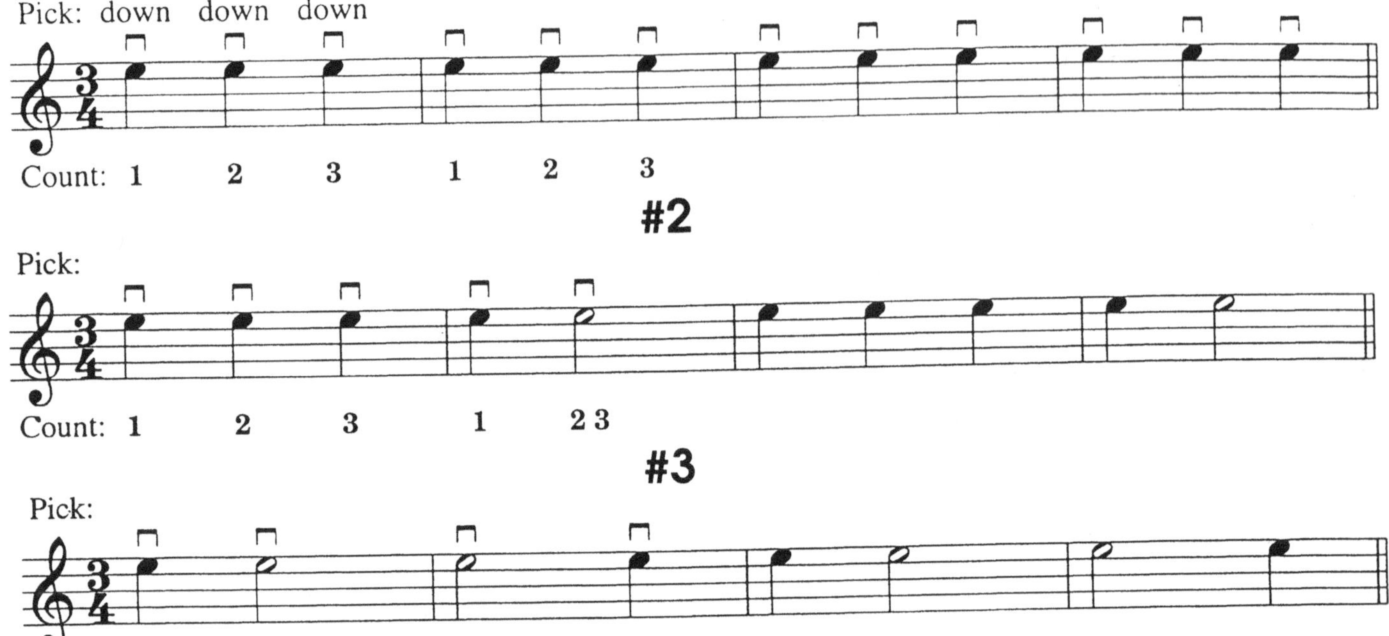

Eighth Note Review/Alternate Picking

Shown below are eighth notes and their time values:

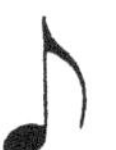

Eighth Notes get 1/2 beat if the bottom number of the time signature is a four.

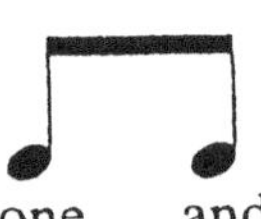

One beat. The beat is divided equally into two parts. Count the first eighth note as the beat in the measure on which it happens, and count the second eighth note as "and."

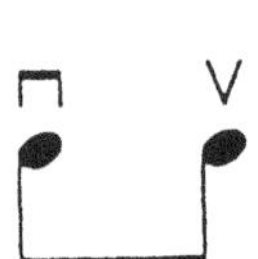

When two eighth notes are connected, the first is played using a downstroke, ⊓ , and the second is played using an upstroke, V . This is called ***alternate picking.*** This technique is used regardless of the position or the string on which the note is played. **Use alternate picking on all eighth notes throughout this book, unless otherwise indicated.** When tapping your foot, the first eighth note is played down when the foot is down, and the second eighth note is played up when the foot is up.

Play the following exercise which contains eighth notes, alternate picking, and the E note on the first string. Be sure to count and tap your foot.

Hiking Up the Mountain

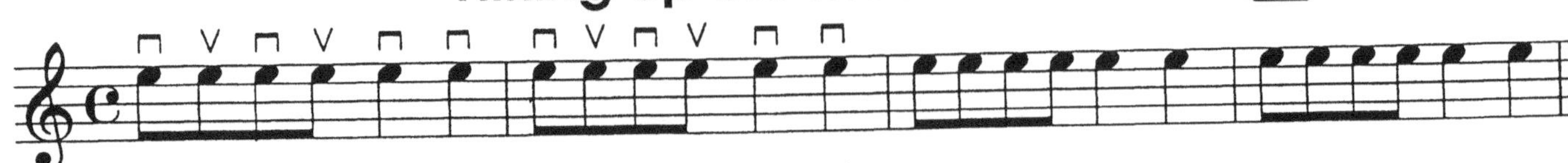

Say: Hi-king up the moun-tain, Hi-king up the moun-tain

Try clapping the rhythm while you say the rhythmic phrase.

Don't Step on Alligators! (Disc 16)

(Say and Play)

Down Down Up Down Up Down Up

Cruising Down the Super Highway (Disc 17)

(Say and Play)

Crui-sing down the empty high-way, etc.

Start Picking Down and Up (Disc 18)

(Say and Play)

Start pick-ing down, and up etc.

A New Note:

F

1st Fret
1st Finger
1st String

Press the fingers down firmly behind the frets. Never place the finger directly on the fretwire.

Note that the numbers of the fret and finger are identical.

E
NUT
F
1
2
3
4
E STRING

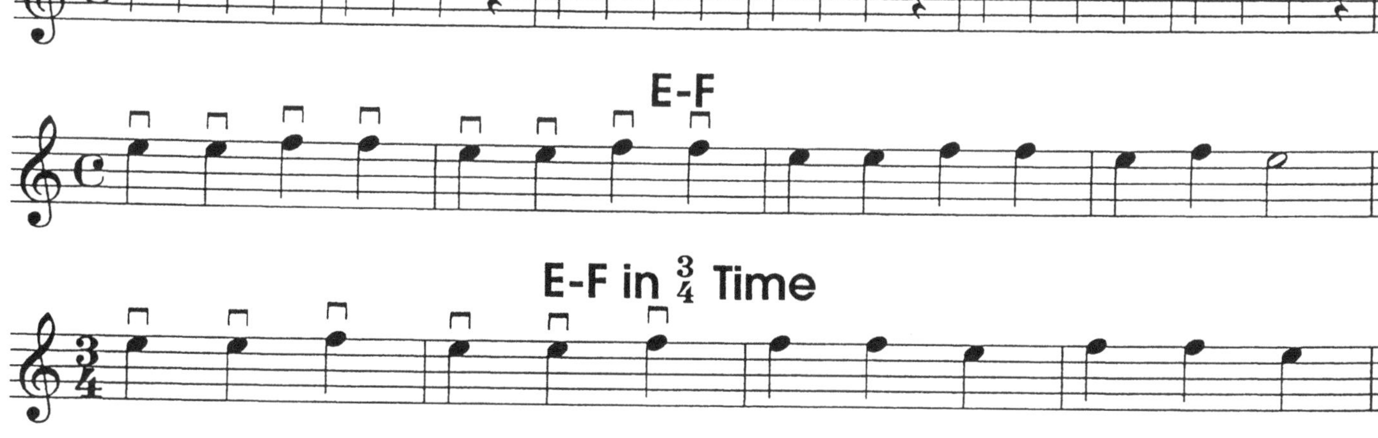

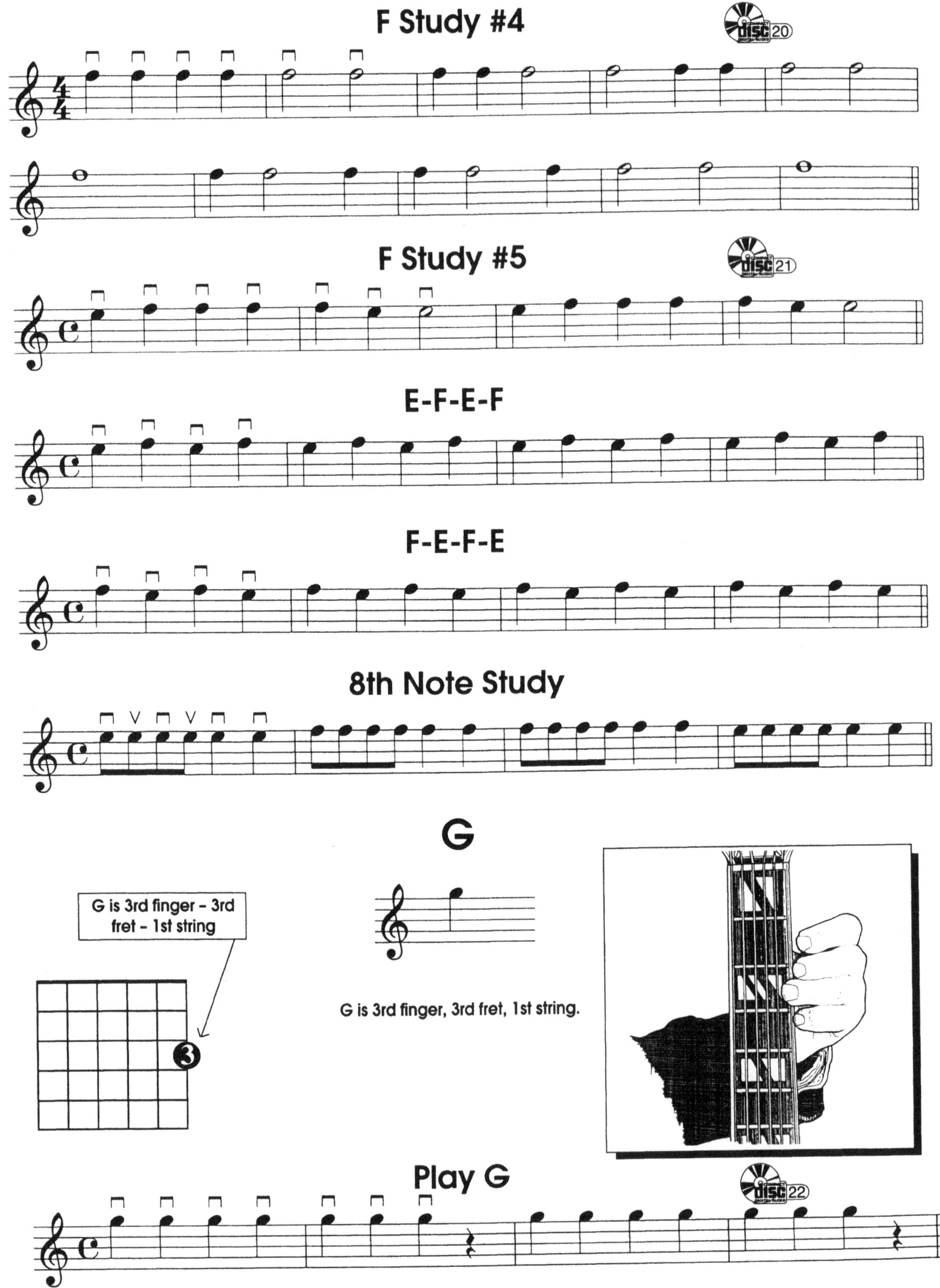
F Study #4
disc 20
F Study #5
disc 21
E-F-E-F
F-E-F-E
8th Note Study
G
G is 3rd finger - 3rd fret - 1st string
3
G is 3rd finger, 3rd fret, 1st string.
Play G
disc 22

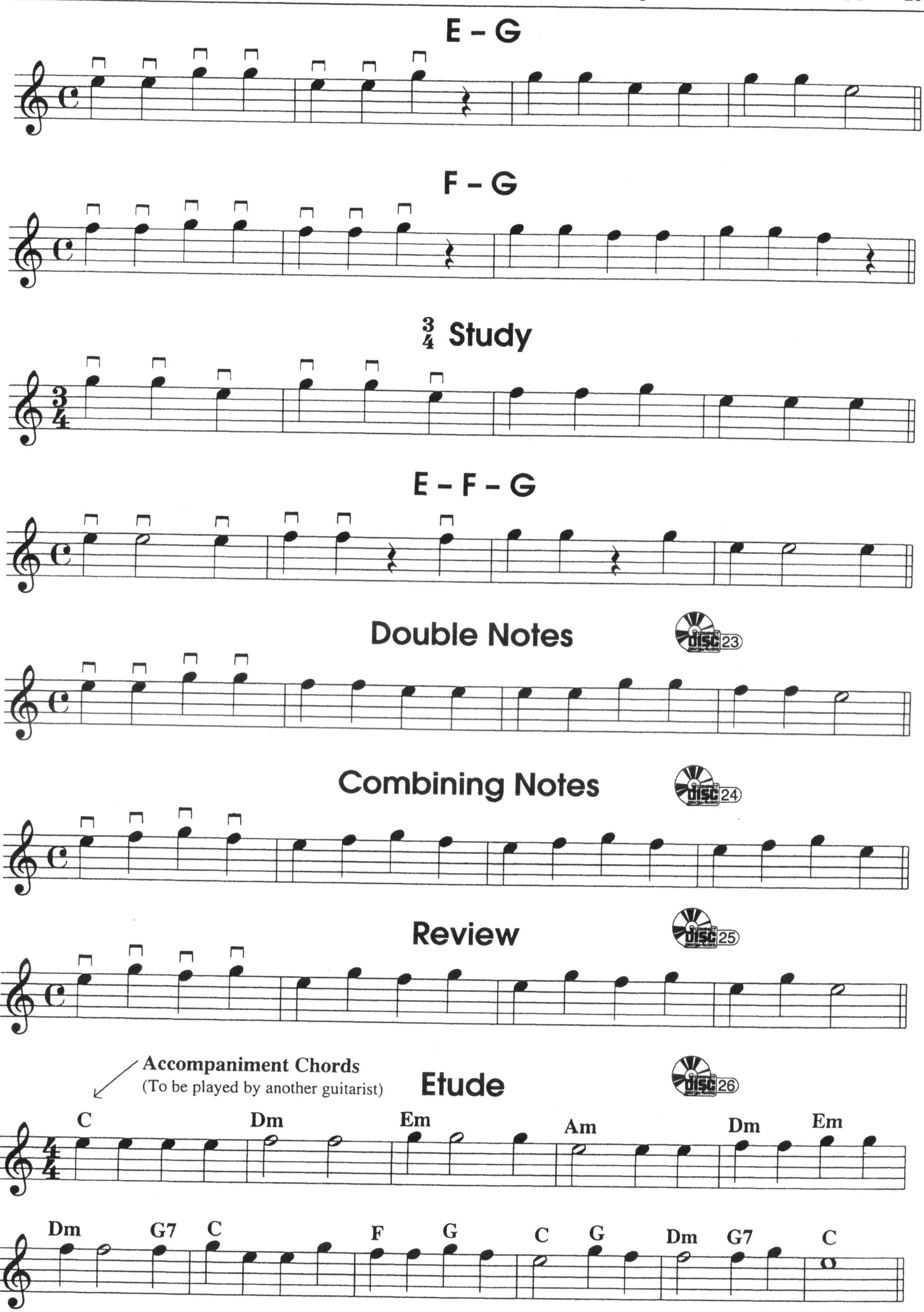
E - G
F - G
3/4 Study
E - F - G
Double Notes
disc 23
Combining Notes
disc 24
Review
disc 25
Accompaniment Chords
(To be played by another guitarist)
Etude
disc 26
C
Dm
Em
Am
Dm
Em
Dm
G7
C
F
G
C
G
Dm
G7
C

1st String Studies

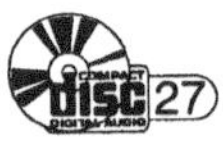

8th Note Rhythm

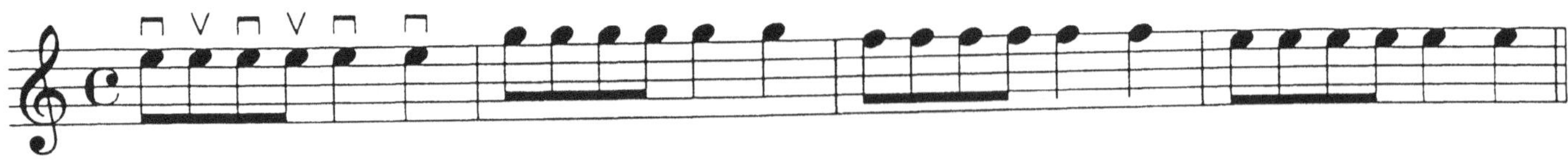

Study #2

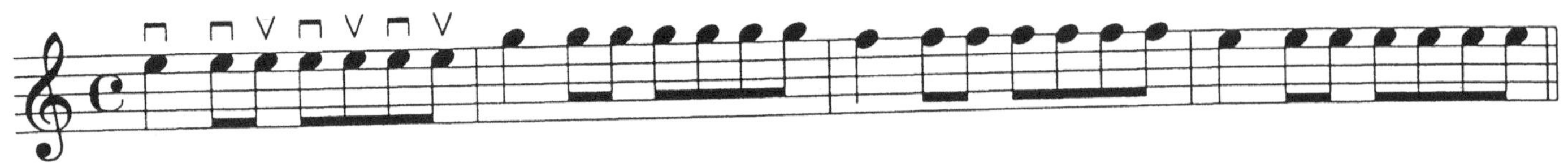

Picking Study

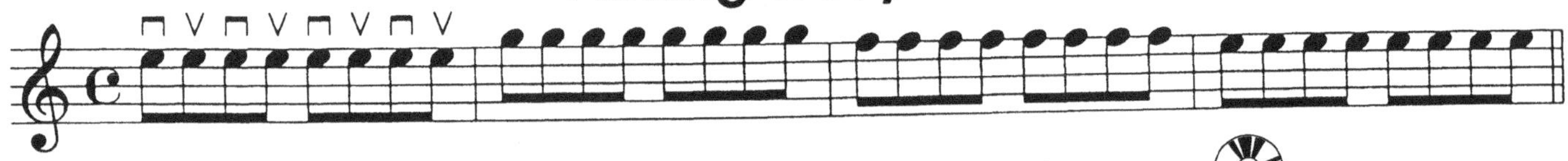

Time and Picking Study

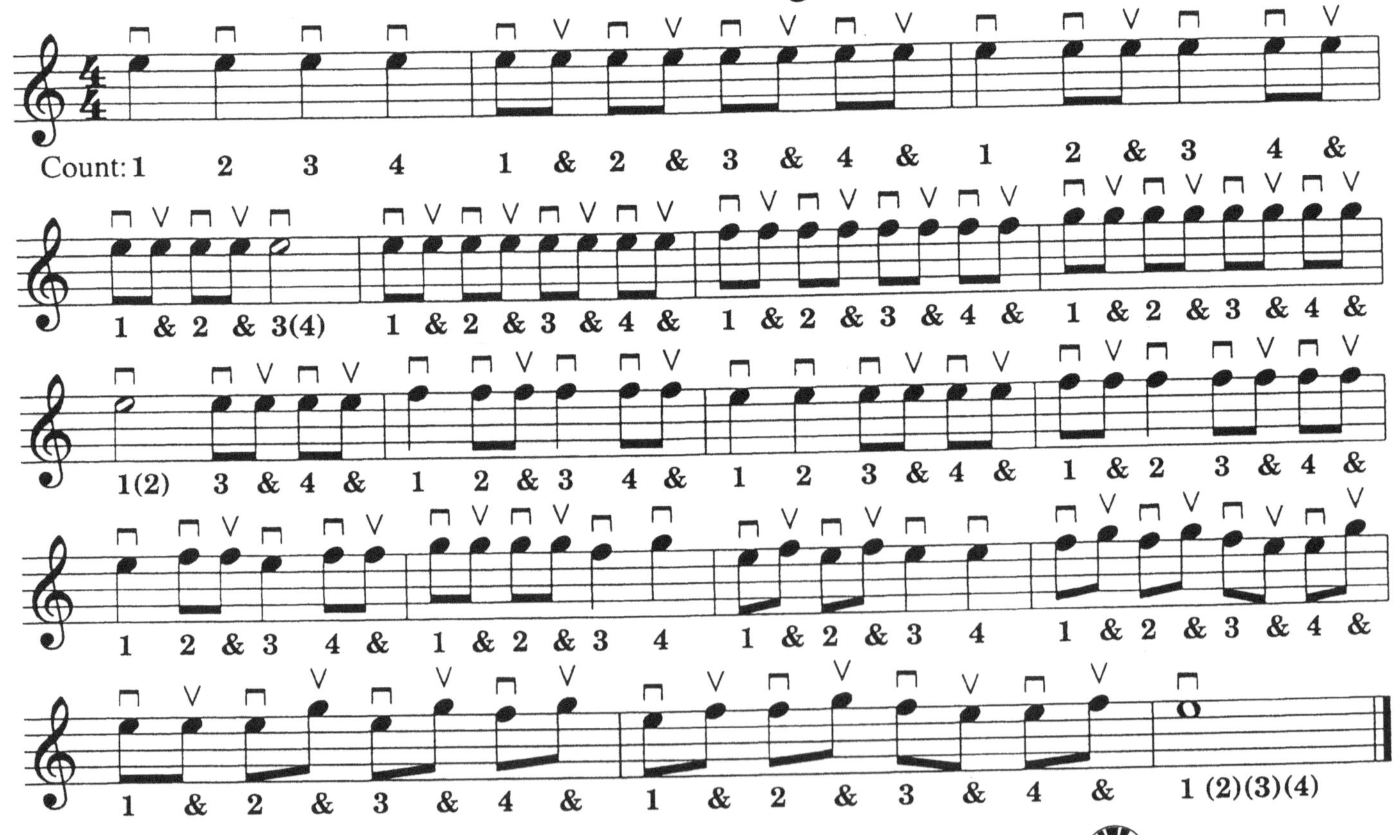

Count: 1 2 3 4 1 & 2 & 3 & 4 & 1 2 & 3 4 &

1 & 2 & 3(4) 1 & 2 & 3 & 4 & 1 & 2 & 3 & 4 & 1 & 2 & 3 & 4 &

1(2) 3 & 4 & 1 2 & 3 4 & 1 2 3 & 4 & 1 & 2 3 & 4 &

1 2 & 3 4 & 1 & 2 & 3 4 1 & 2 & 3 4 1 & 2 & 3 & 4 &

1 & 2 & 3 & 4 & 1 & 2 & 3 & 4 & 1 (2)(3)(4)

Play Slowly

Speed Study

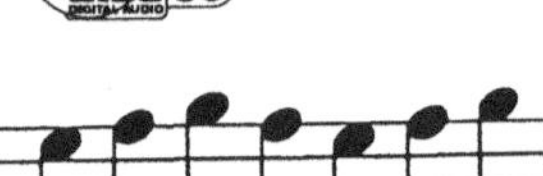

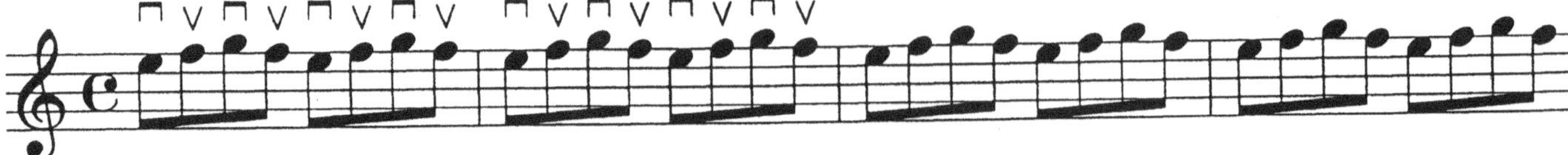

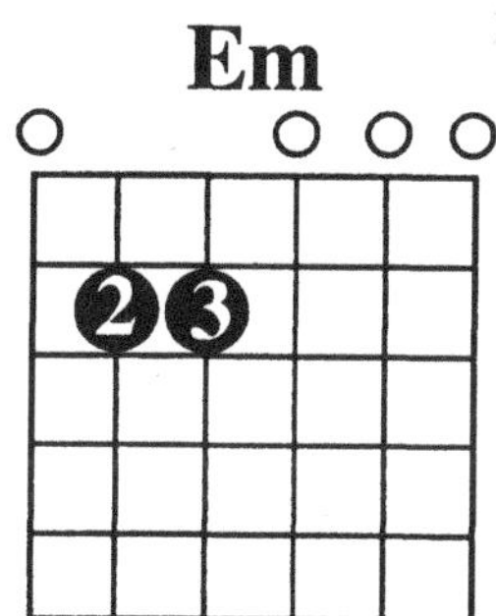

E Minor

The chord drawn at left is E minor. **Minor** chords are written with an ***m*** or a ***dash (-)*** next to the chord letter name.

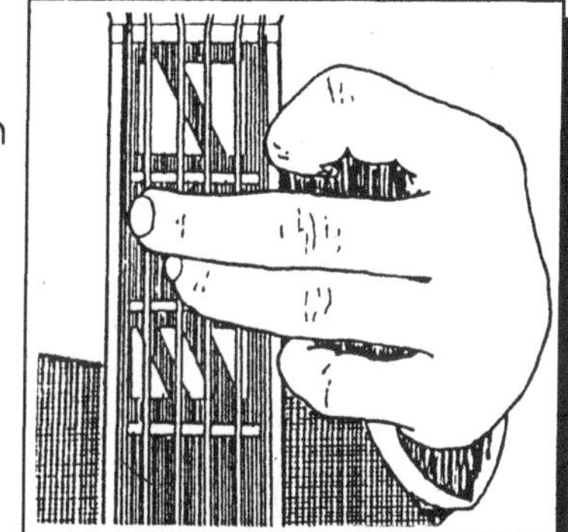

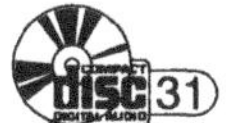

Practice the following exercise which contains E minor.

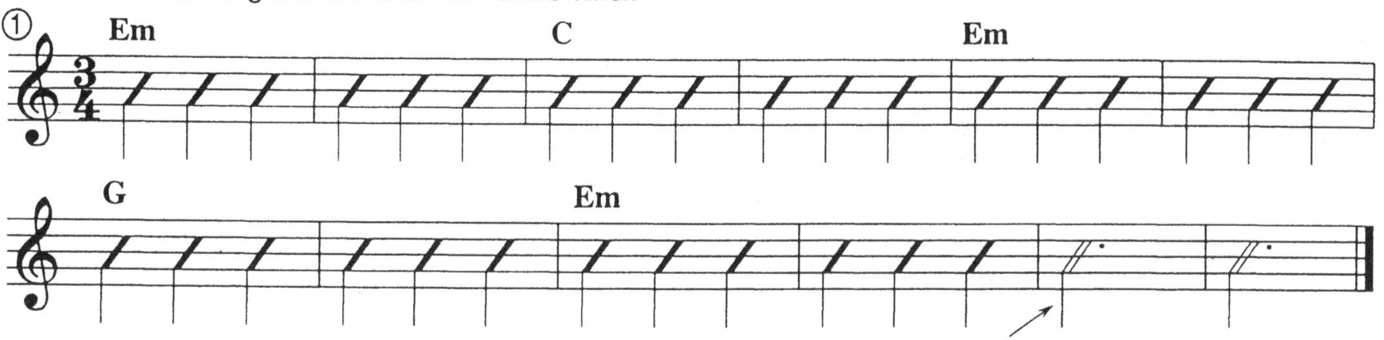

D

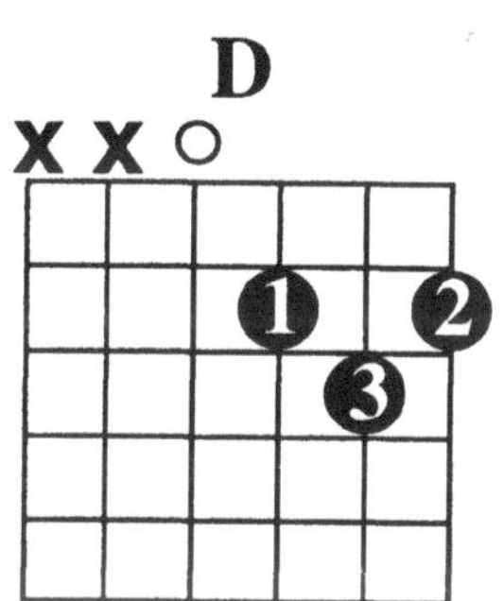

Drawn at left is the **D chord.** Practice getting a clear sound out of each of the strings in a D chord. Notice only four strings are played.

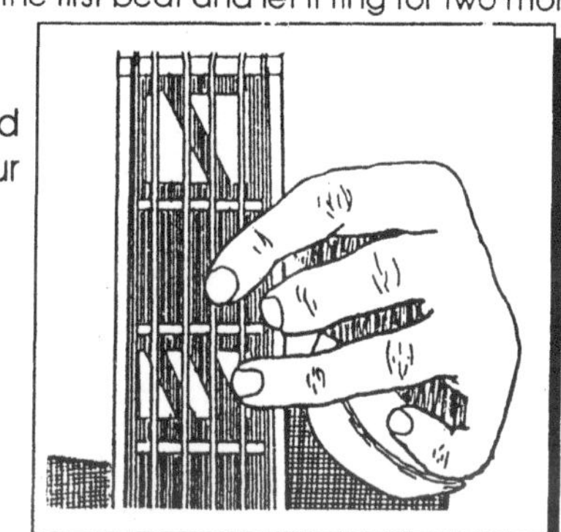

Practice the following exercises which contain some D chords. Notice the use of rests in this exercise.

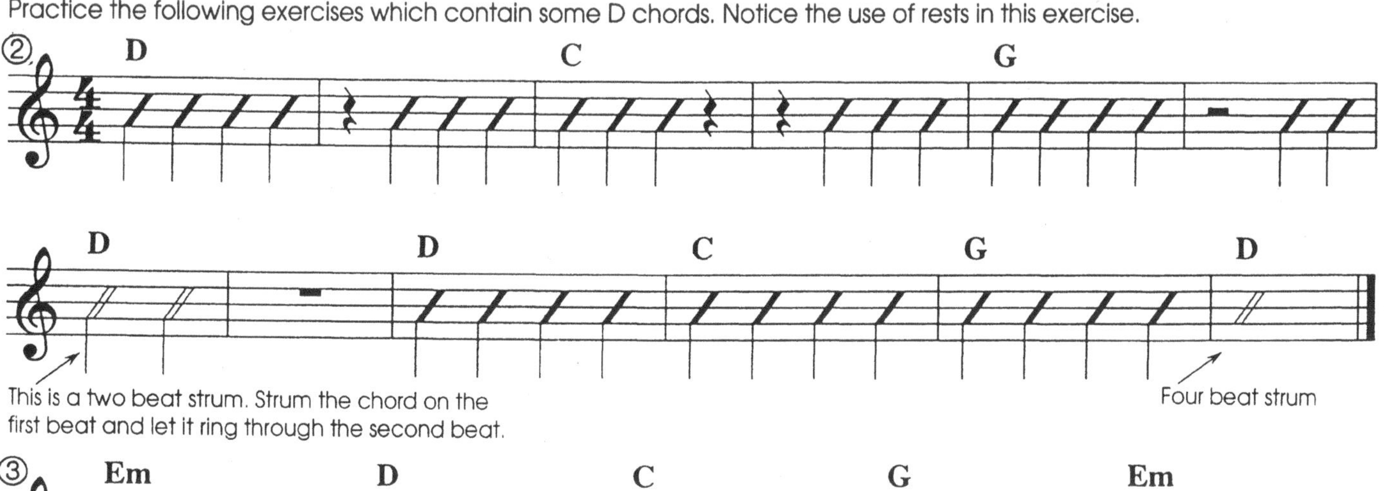

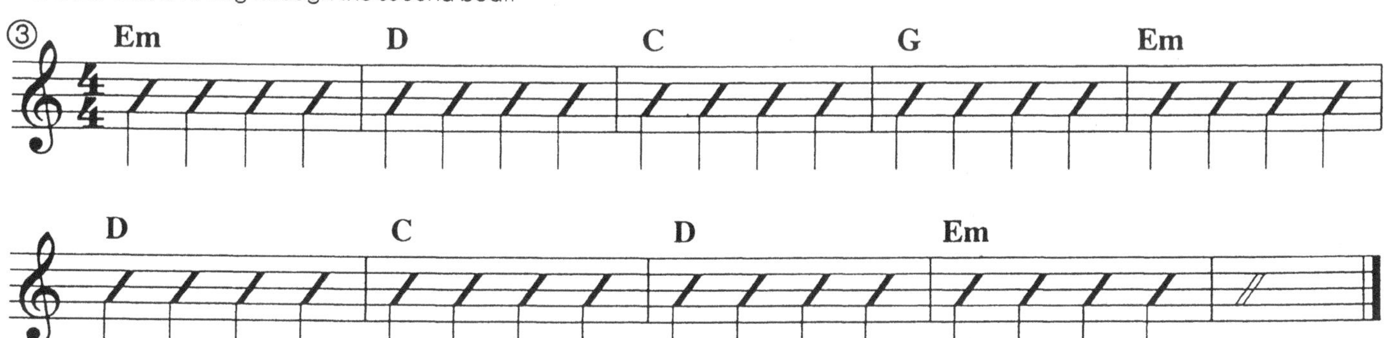

Practice the following songs using the chords you have learned so far. Above the first measure in each song is written the number of times to strum in each measure.

The Cuckoo

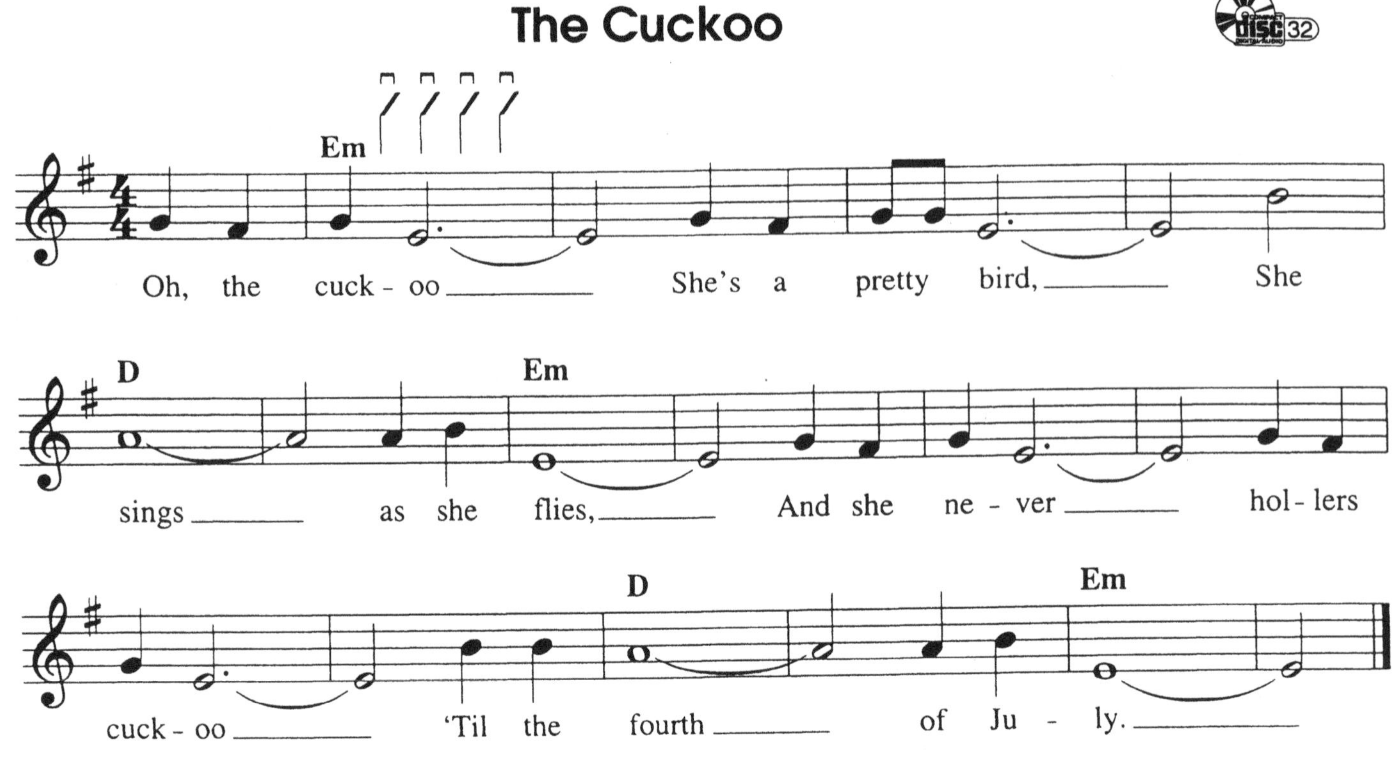

> : This is an ***accent mark***. When it is placed above a note or a strum bar, play that note or strum slightly louder.

Sweet Sunny South

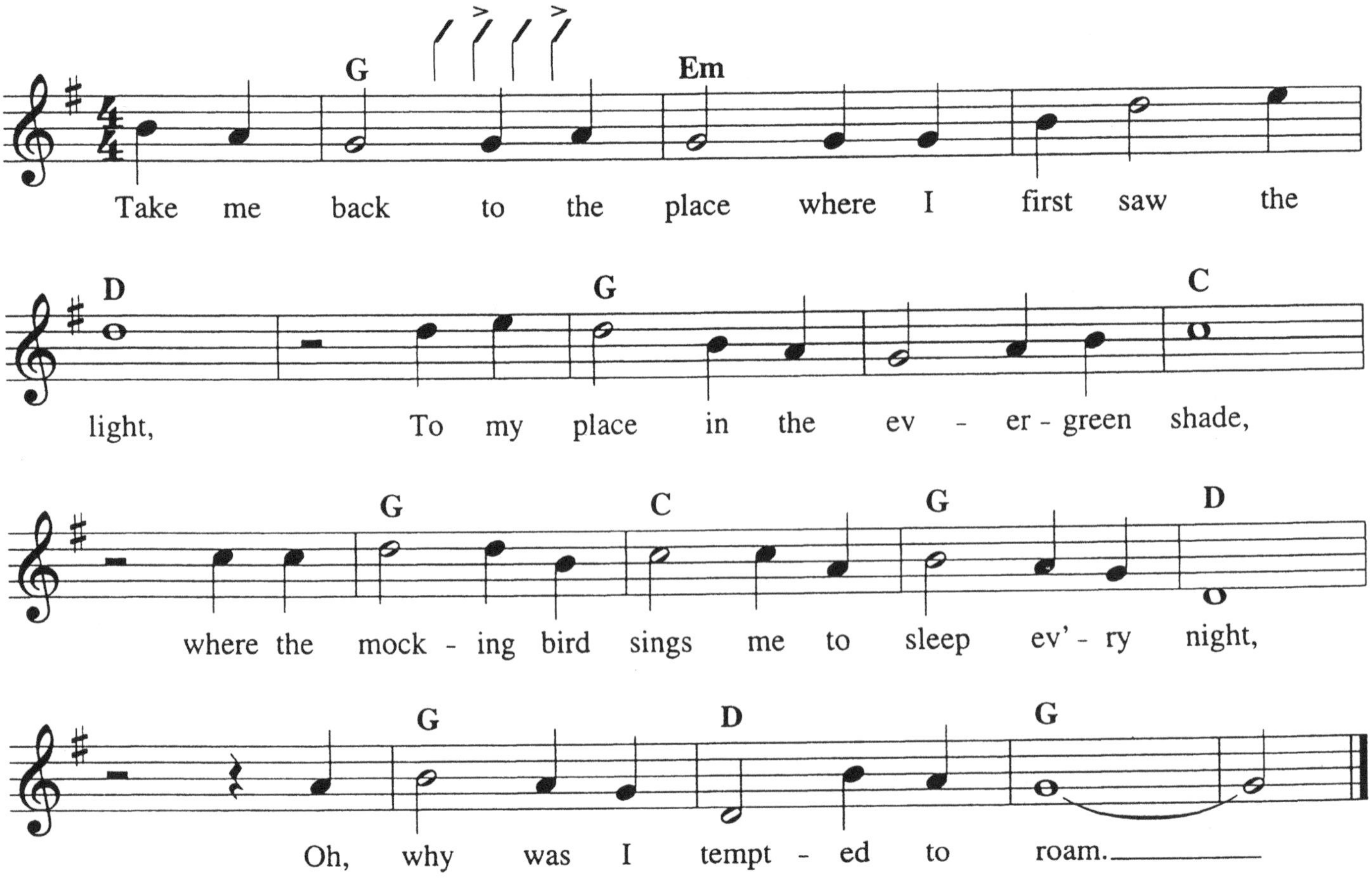

33

G Em

Take me back to the place where I first saw the

D G C

light, To my place in the ev - er - green shade,

G C G D

where the mock - ing bird sings me to sleep ev' - ry night,

G D G

Oh, why was I tempt - ed to roam.

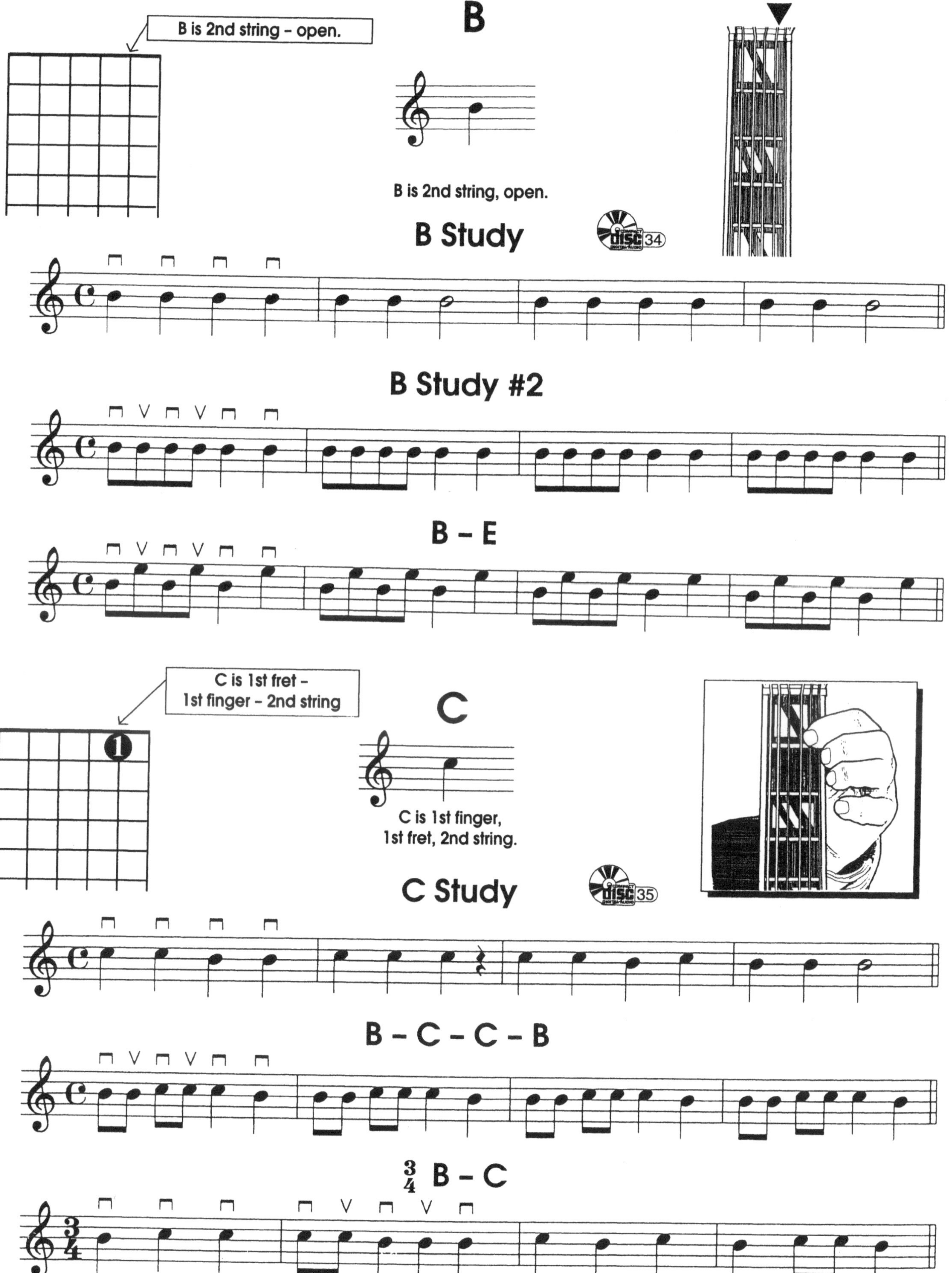
B is 2nd string - open.
B
B is 2nd string, open.
B Study
disc 34
B Study #2
B - E
C is 1st fret -
1st finger - 2nd string
1
C
C is 1st finger,
1st fret, 2nd string.
C Study
disc 35
B - C - C - B
3/4 B - C

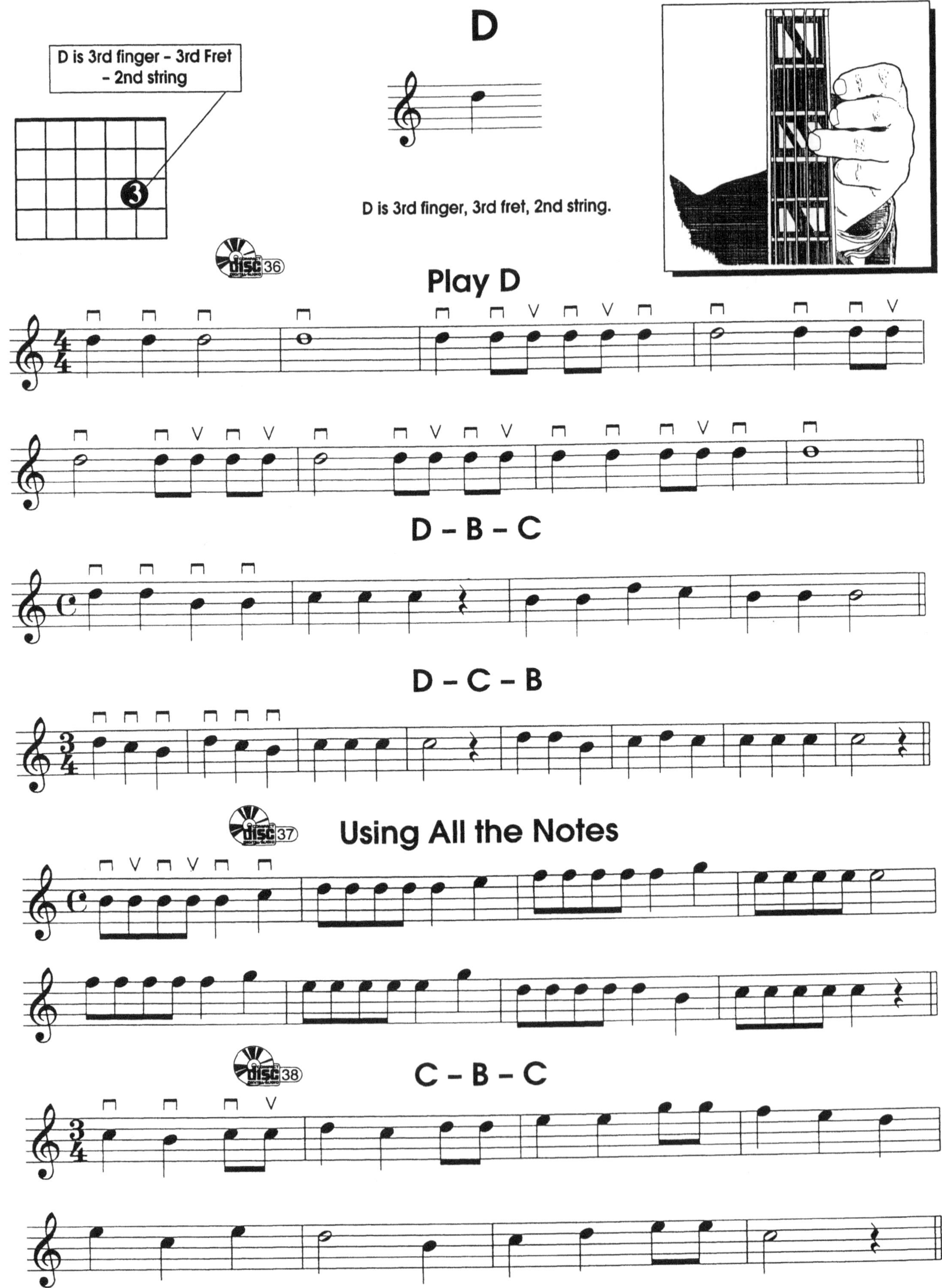
D
D is 3rd finger - 3rd Fret - 2nd string
3
D is 3rd finger, 3rd fret, 2nd string.
disc 36
Play D
D - B - C
D - C - B
disc 37
Using All the Notes
disc 38
C - B - C

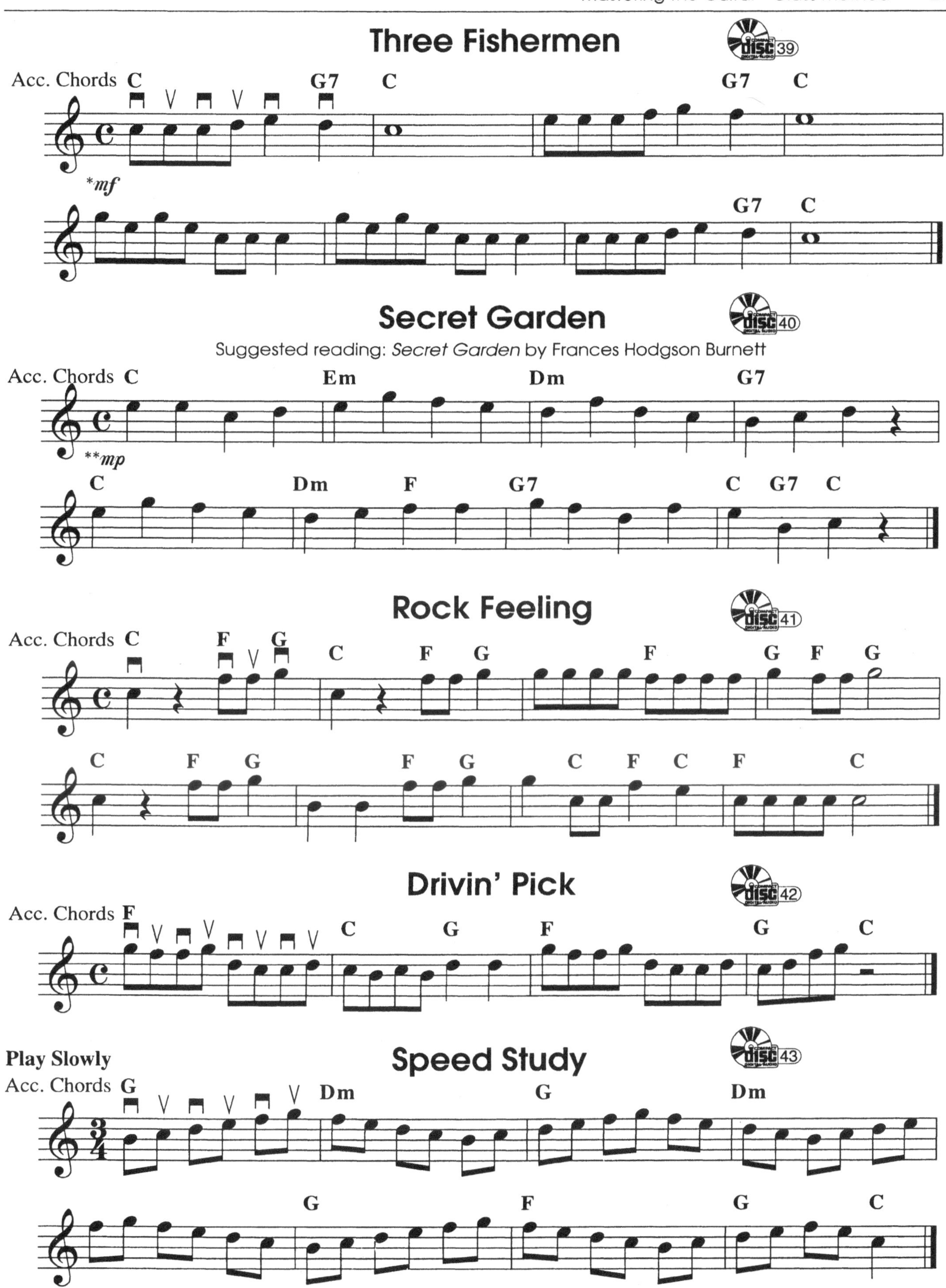

*mf mezzo forte - medium loud

**mp mezzo piano - medium soft

The Tie

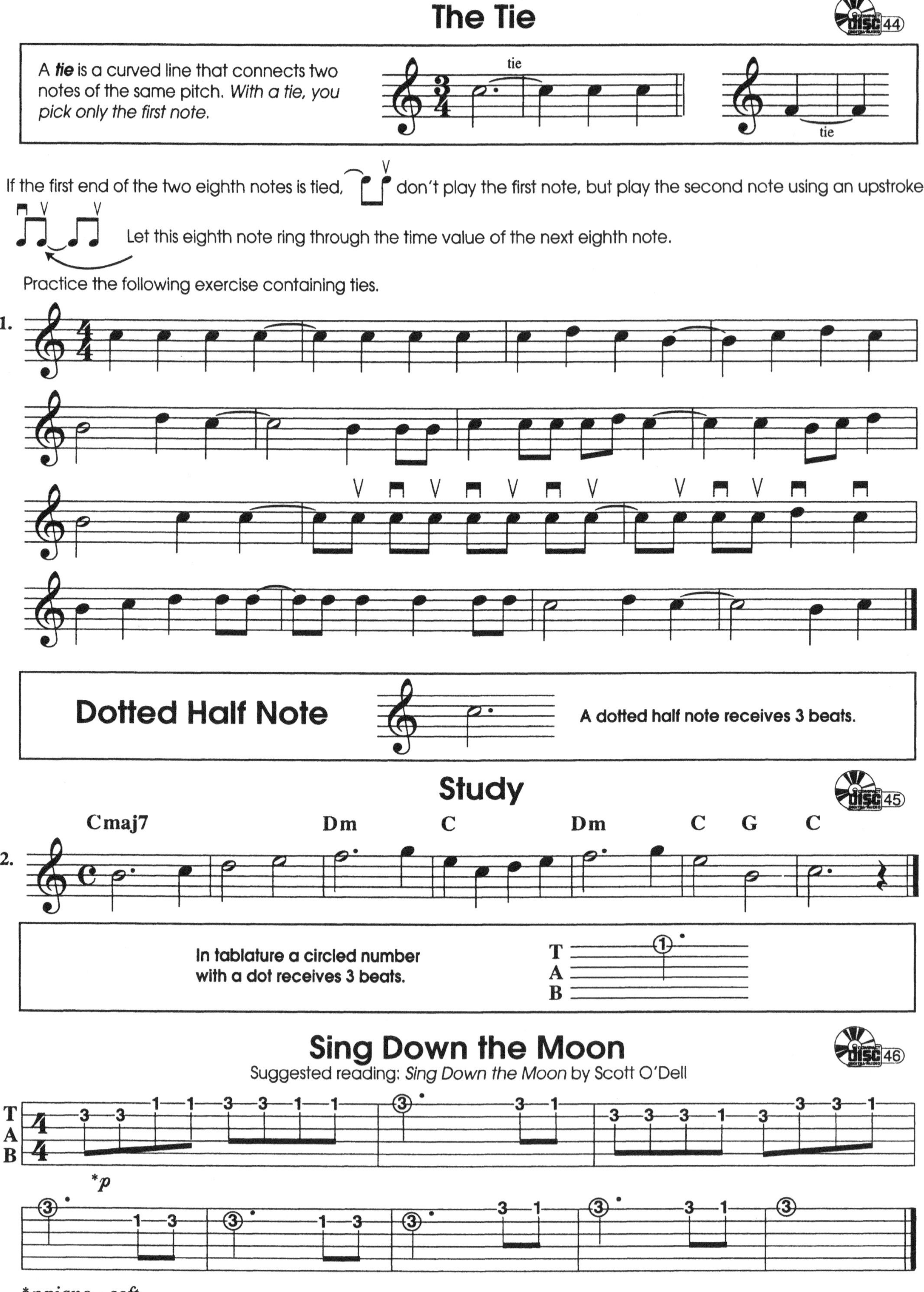

A ***tie*** is a curved line that connects two notes of the same pitch. *With a tie, you pick only the first note.*

If the first end of the two eighth notes is tied, don't play the first note, but play the second note using an upstroke.

Let this eighth note ring through the time value of the next eighth note.

Practice the following exercise containing ties.

Dotted Half Note

A dotted half note receives 3 beats.

Study

In tablature a circled number with a dot receives 3 beats.

Sing Down the Moon

Suggested reading: *Sing Down the Moon* by Scott O'Dell

**p* *piano - soft*

Musical Math Quiz

Grade __________

Write the answers to the following addition problems.

1. 𝅗𝅥 + 𝅗𝅥 =
2. 𝅗𝅥 + 𝅗𝅥. =
3. 𝅝 + 𝅗𝅥 =
4. 𝅗𝅥. + ♩ =
5. 𝅗𝅥. + 𝅗𝅥. =
6. 𝅝 + 𝅗𝅥. =
7. 𝅗𝅥. + 𝅗𝅥 =
8. 𝅝 + 𝅝 =
9. 𝅗𝅥. + 𝅝 =
10. 𝅝 + ♩ =
11. ♩ + ♩ + 𝅗𝅥 =
12. 𝅗𝅥 + ♩ + 𝅗𝅥. =
13. 𝅗𝅥. + 𝅗𝅥 + ♩ =
14. ♩ + 𝅝 + 𝅗𝅥 =
15. 𝅝 + 𝅗𝅥. + ♩ =
16. 𝅗𝅥. + ♩ + 𝅗𝅥 =
17. ♩ + 𝅝 + ♩ =
18. 𝅝 + 𝅗𝅥. + 𝅝 =

Notes on the 3rd String

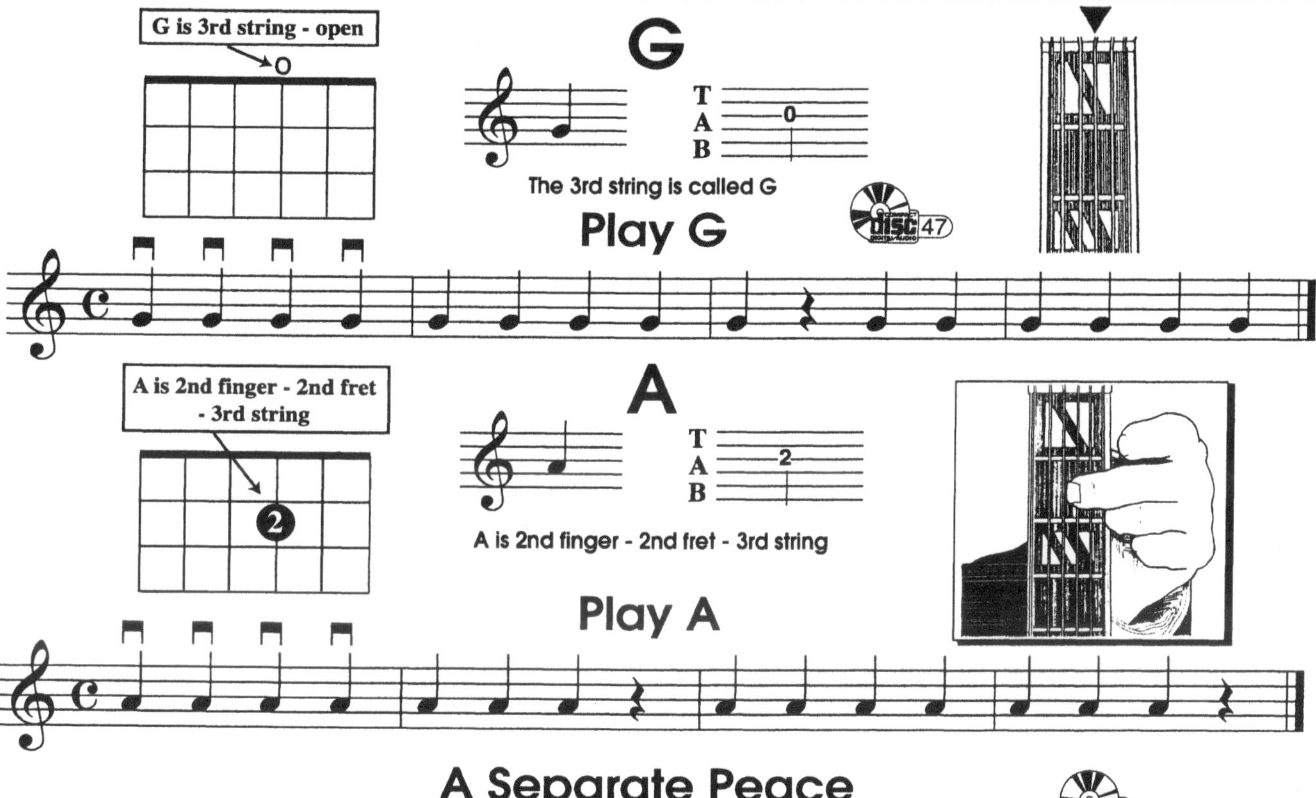

A Separate Peace

Suggested reading: *A Separate Peace* by John Knowles

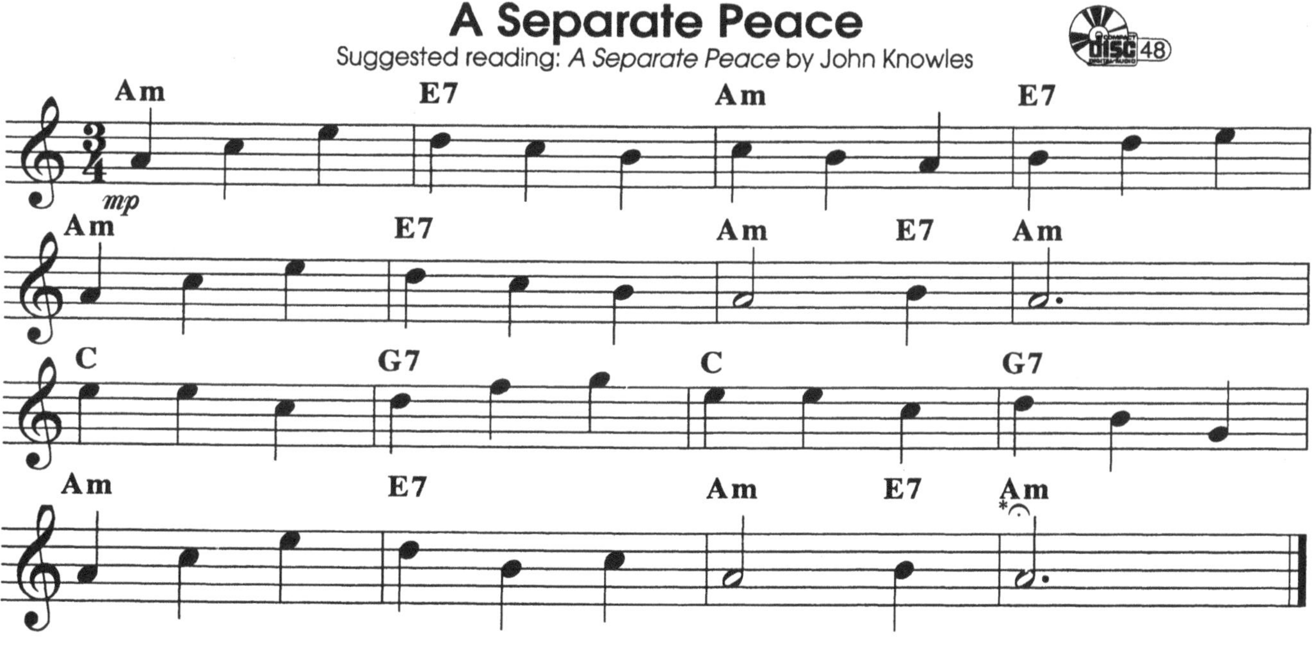

*𝄐 *fermata - pause, hold*

Full G, G7, and C Chords

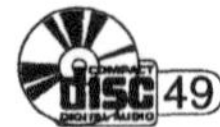

Drawn below are the full **G, G7, and C chords.** These full chords will sound better than the simple chords and should be used from here on throughout this book. To get a clear sound out of each string, keep the knuckles square and use the tips of the fingers. On the G chord, the numbers in parenthesis are an optional fingering.

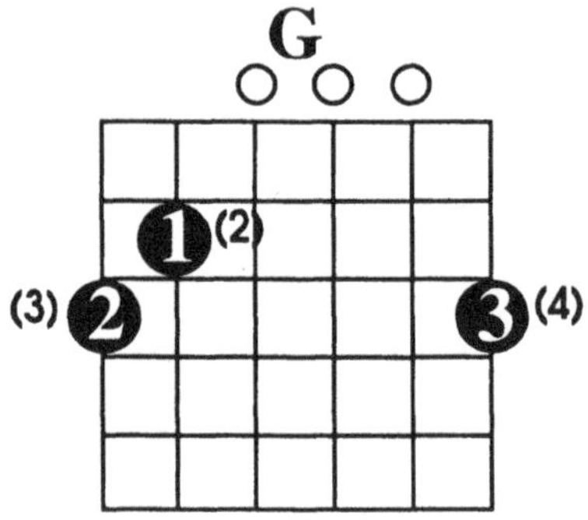

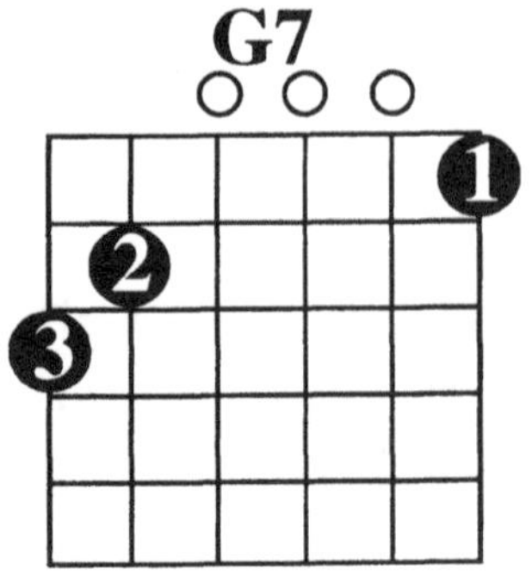

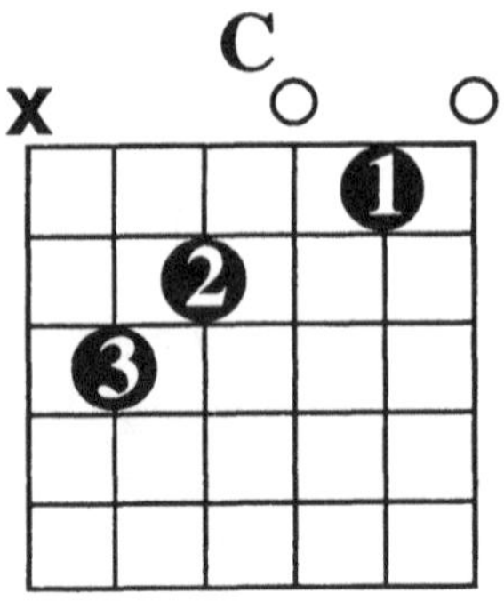

G G7 C

Practice the following exercises using full chords.

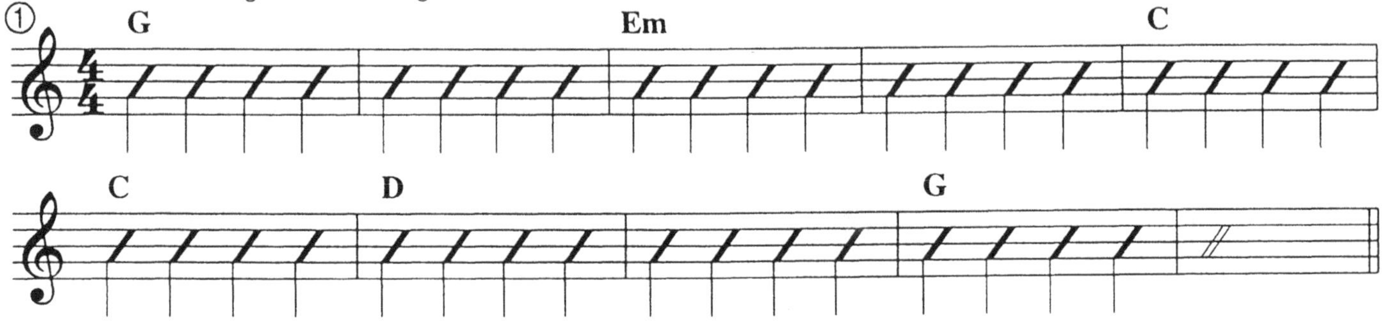

① G Em C

C D G

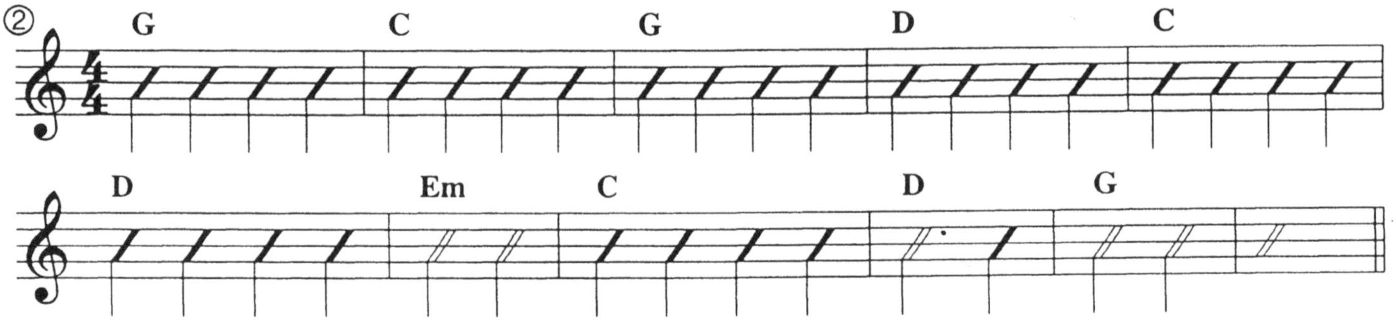

② G C G D C

D Em C D G

Practice strumming the chords to the following song using full chords.

disc 50

Will the Circle Be Unbroken?

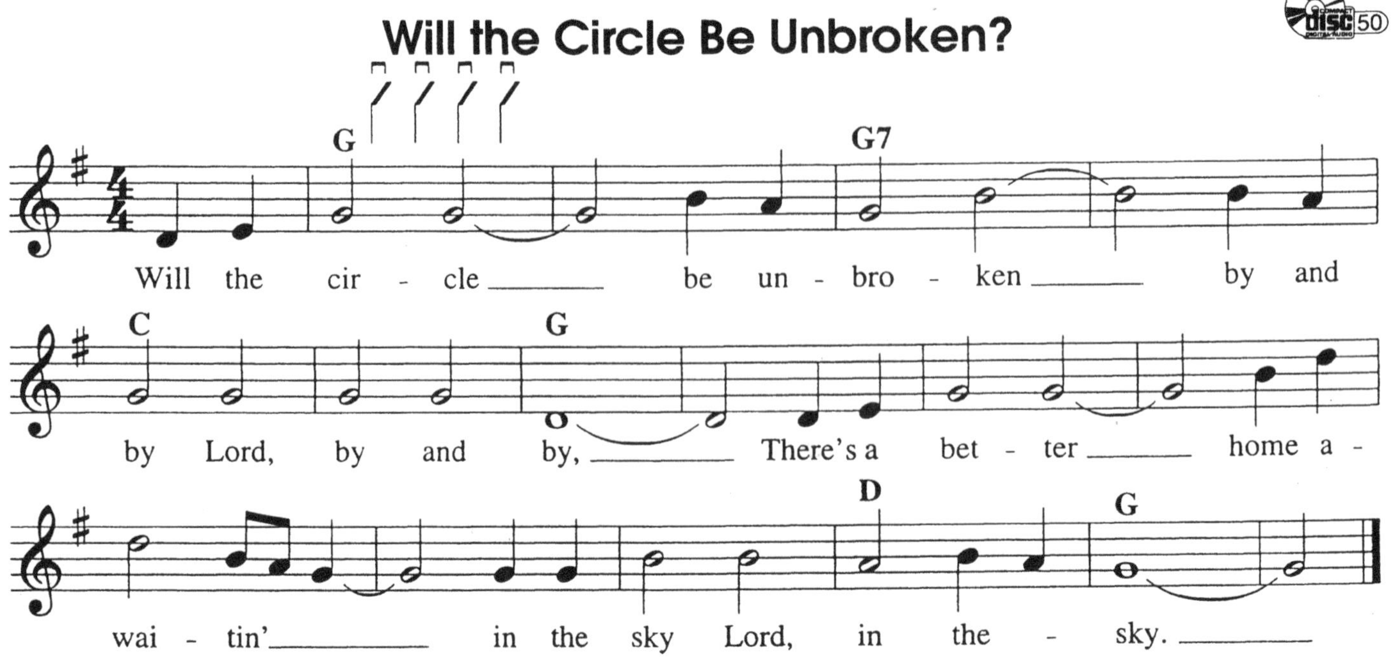

Strum Patterns

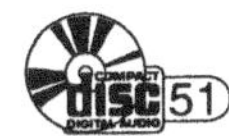

Like eighth notes, when two strum bars are connected with a beam, ⌐/⌐/, two strums are played in one beat. Usually, the first strum is down, and the second is strummed up, ⊓ V. The down-up strum is counted the same as two eighth notes (i.e. "one-and"). As with the down strums, the strumming may be done with a pick, the right-hand thumb, or the first finger. When strumming up, only the first (smallest) two or three strings should be strummed. The up strum is done quickly with an up and outward motion.

Practice the following using down-up strums.

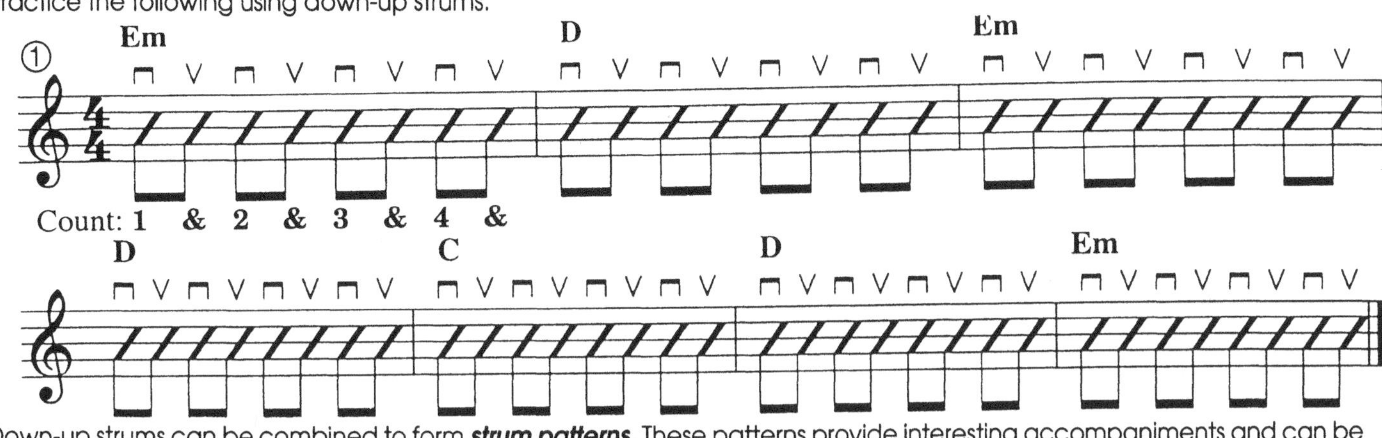

Down-up strums can be combined to form ***strum patterns.*** These patterns provide interesting accompaniments and can be used to play many songs. One pattern which can be used to accompany songs in 4/4 is: ⊓ ⊓V ⊓ ⊓.

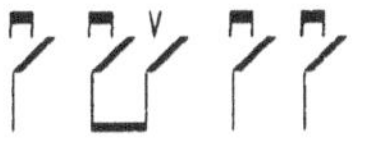

This pattern can be used to play each measure of any song in 4/4. The songs and exercises in this book which are to be strummed will have strum patterns written above (or in) the first measure. That pattern should be used in each measure of the song, unless otherwise indicated. It's important to realize that these patterns can not only be used to play the songs in this book, but they can also be applied to songs in 4/4 and 3/4 from sheet music and/or songbooks.

Practice the following exercise and song repeating the strum pattern which is written above (or in) the first measure.

② Use this pattern in each measure. This pattern can be used to play songs in 4/4.

G | Em | G

Count: 1 2 & 3 4

D | G | D | G

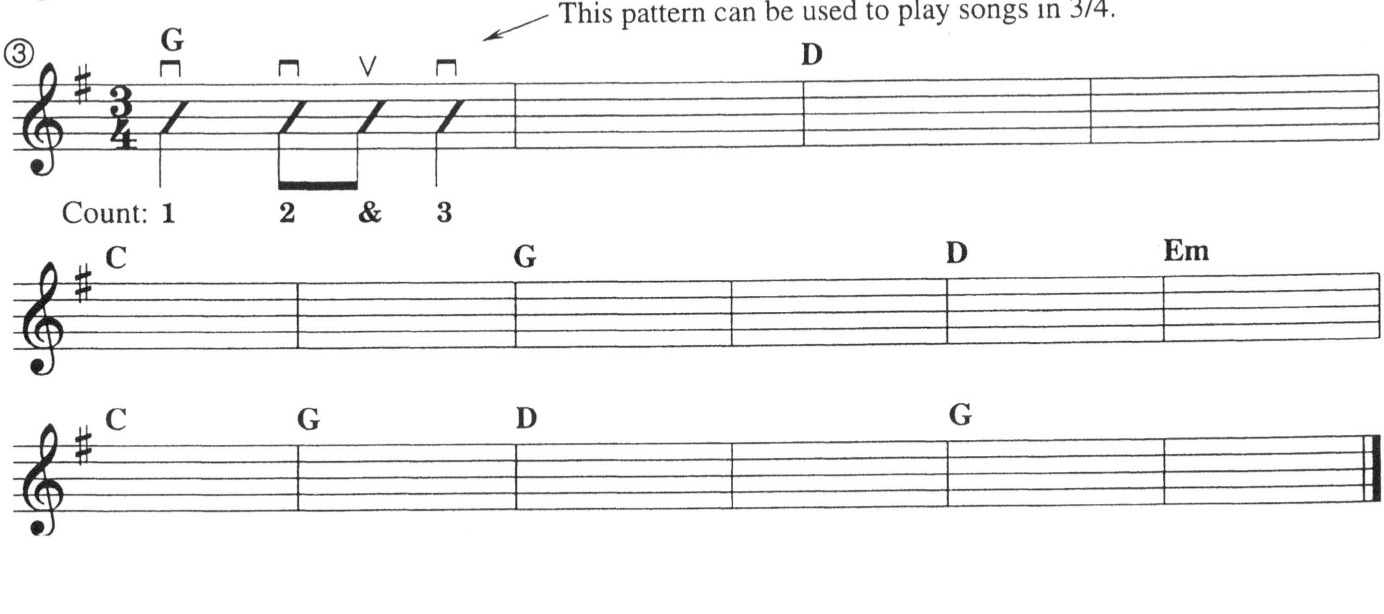

③ This pattern can be used to play songs in 3/4.

G | D

Count: 1 2 & 3

C | G | D | Em

C | G | D | G

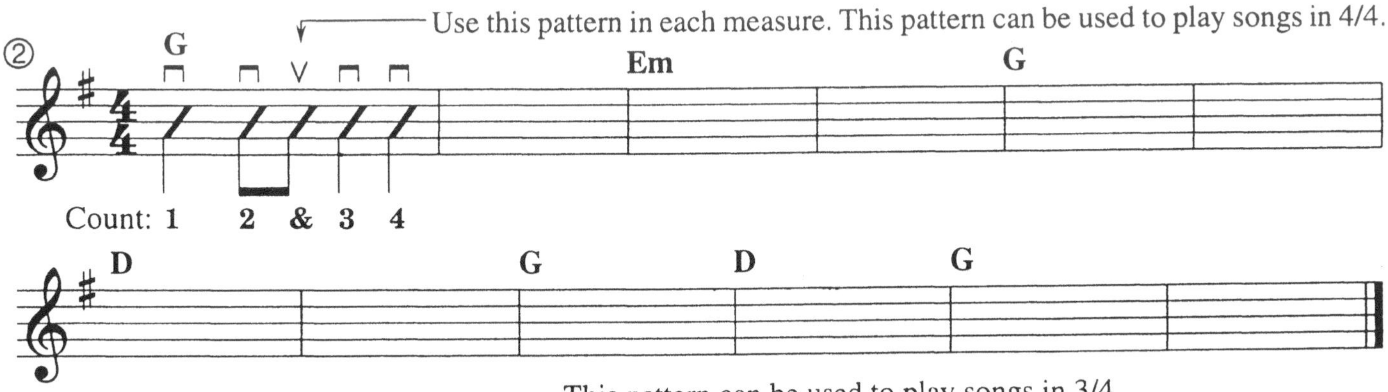

Swing Rhythm

When strumming chords, it is common to play eighth note strums (two strums to a beat) using *swing rhythm*. When playing swing rhythm, rather than divide each beat into two equal parts, the beat is divided into a long-short pattern:

Long (2/3 beat) → ← **Short** (1/3 beat)

The down strum note gets about 2/3 of the beat and the up strum gets about 1/3 of the beat. This rhythm gives the music a bouncy feel. To get the feel of this rhythm, think of the melody to the "Battle Hymn of the Republic." This song is often sung with a swing feel.

Power chords, which are presented later in this book, are often played using swing rhythm.

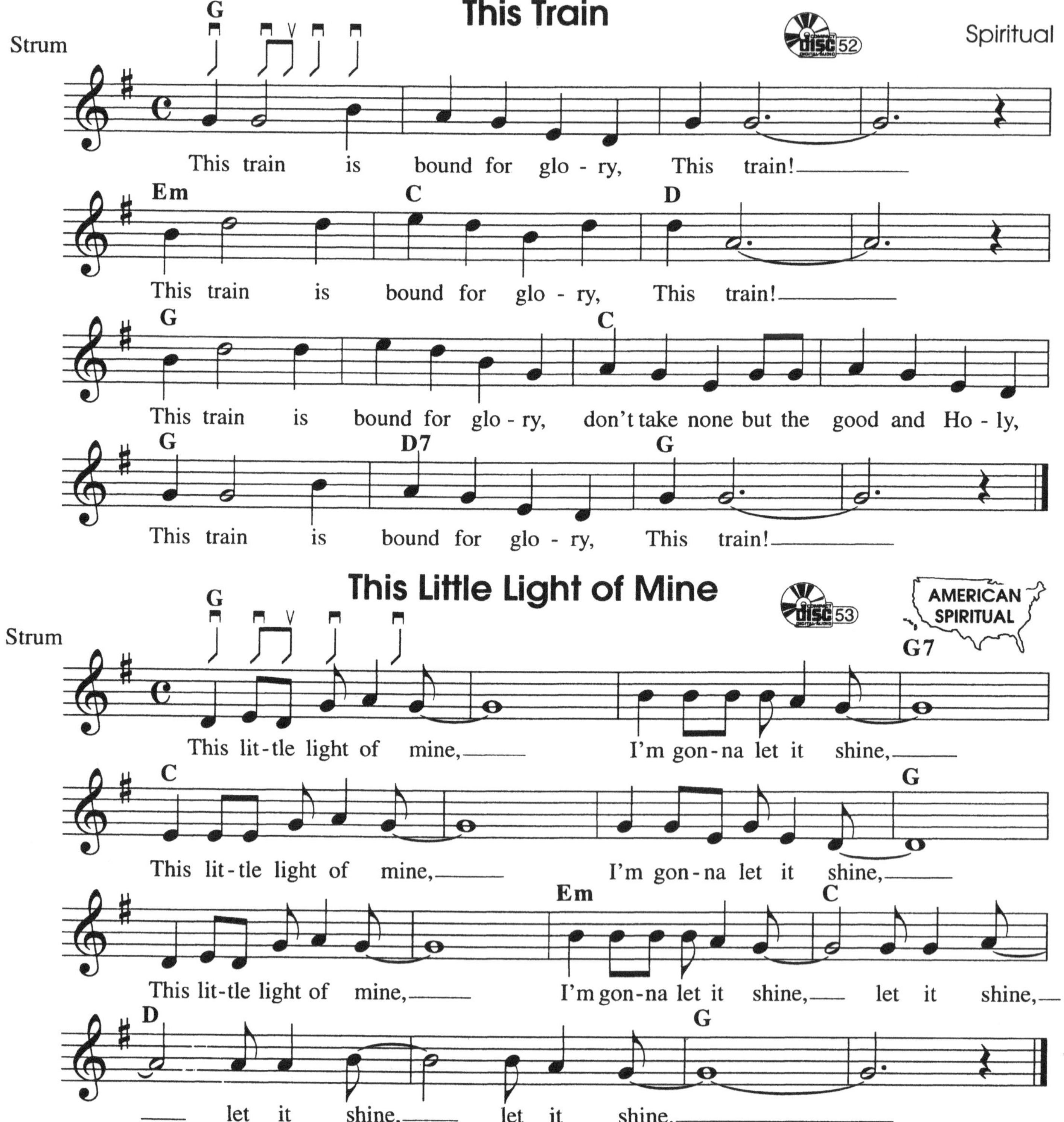

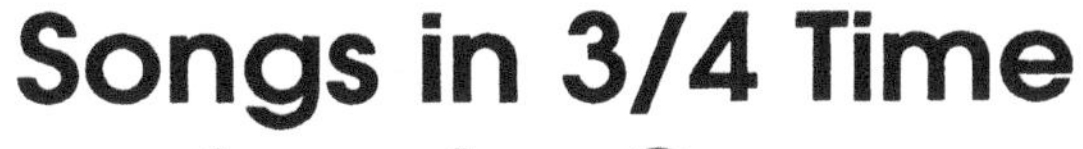

Songs in 3/4 Time

Amazing Grace

Hymn

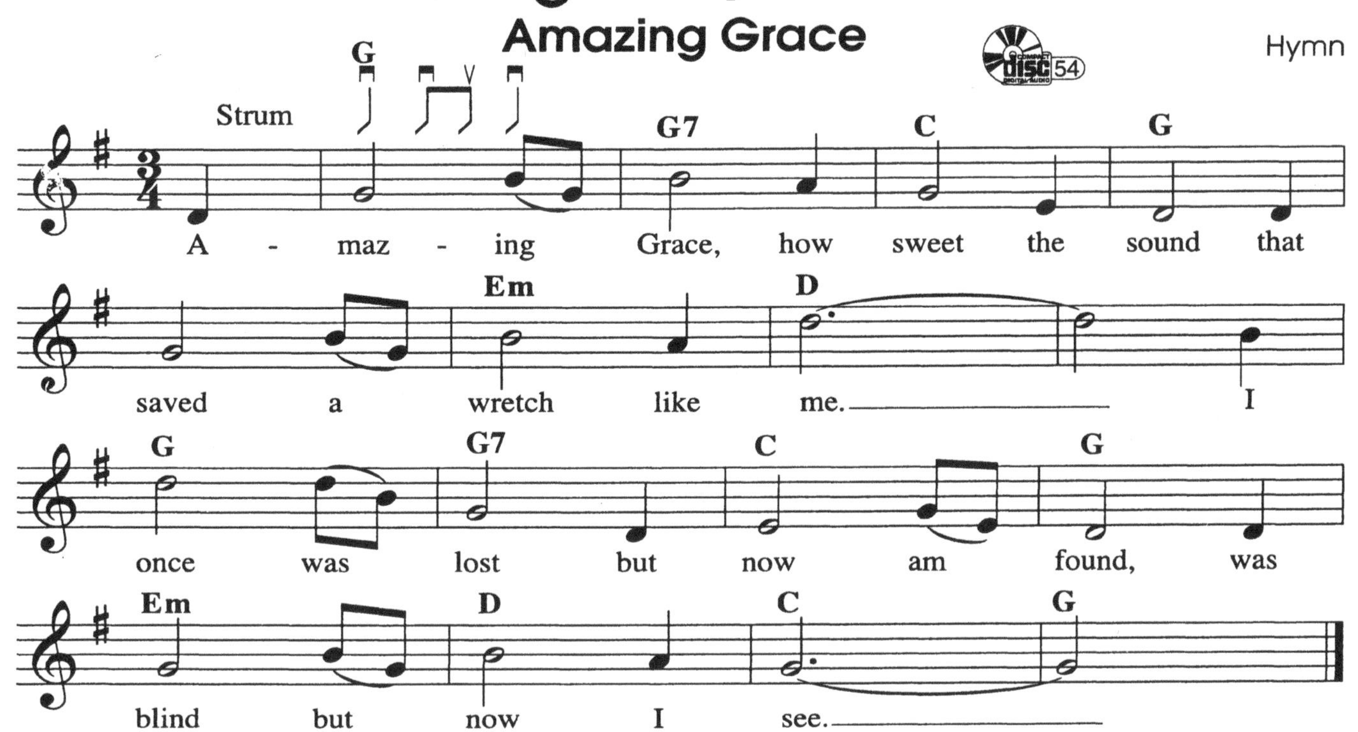

The Railroad Corral

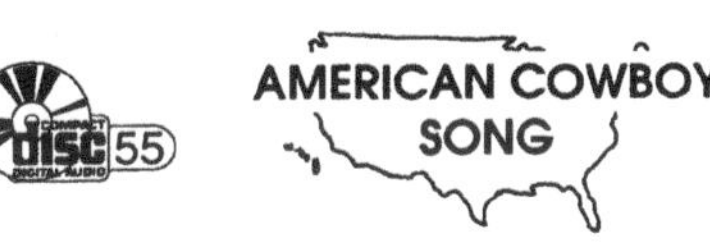

Written in 1904 by Joseph Mills Hansen and based on the tune of a Scottish ballad called "Bonnie Dundee."

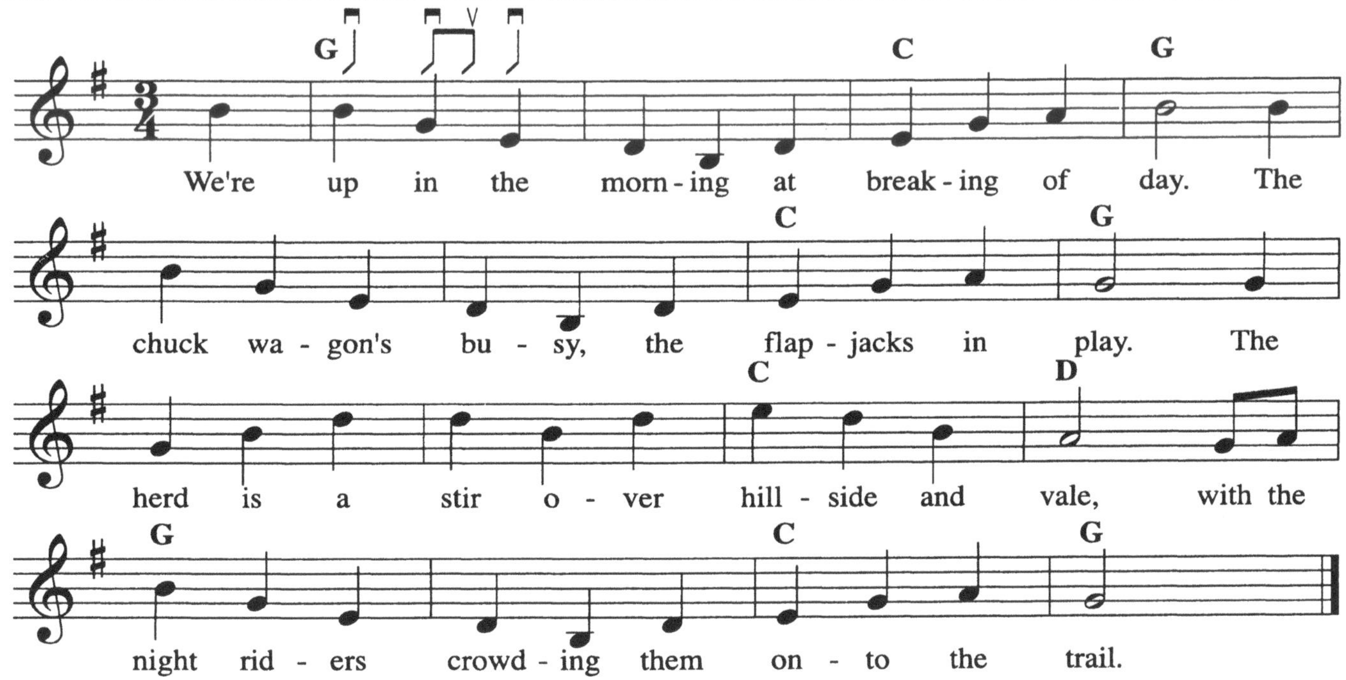

Dialect: Regional variety of language.

chuck wagon	bronco
flapjacks	roust
cinches	chaparral
reins	corral

CHORUS: Come take up your cinches and shake out your reins, (G C G)
Come wake your old bronco and break for the plains. (C G)
Come roust out your steers from the long chaparral, (C D)
For the outfit is off to the railroad corral. (G C G)

A Wrinkle In Time

Guitar Ensemble in Three Parts

Suggested reading: *A Wrinkle In Time* by Madeleine L' Engle

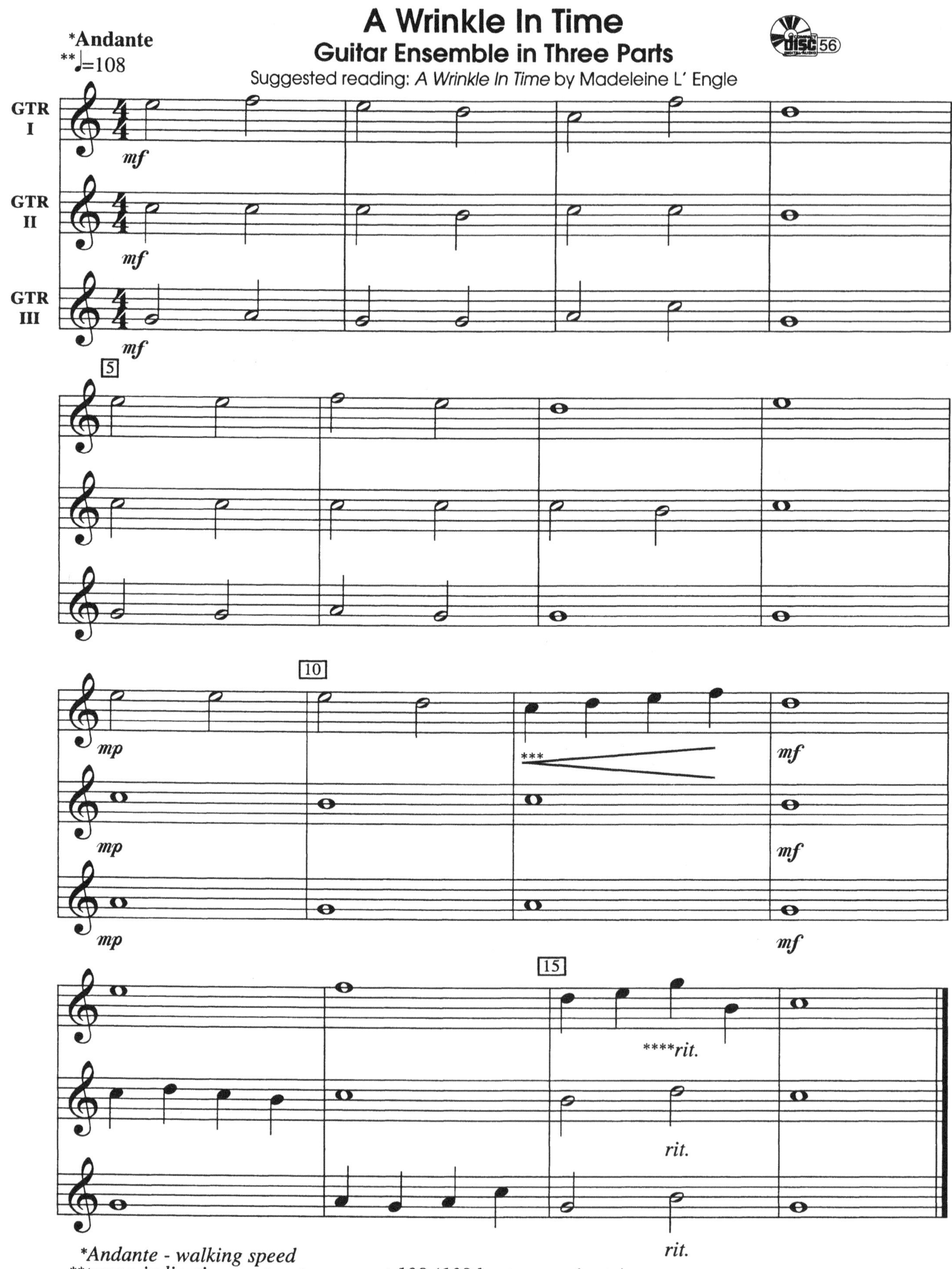

**Andante - walking speed*
***tempo indication - set metronome at 108 (108 beats per minute)*
****crescendo - gradually get louder*
*****ritardando (rit.) - gradually get slower*

Review of the First 3 Strings

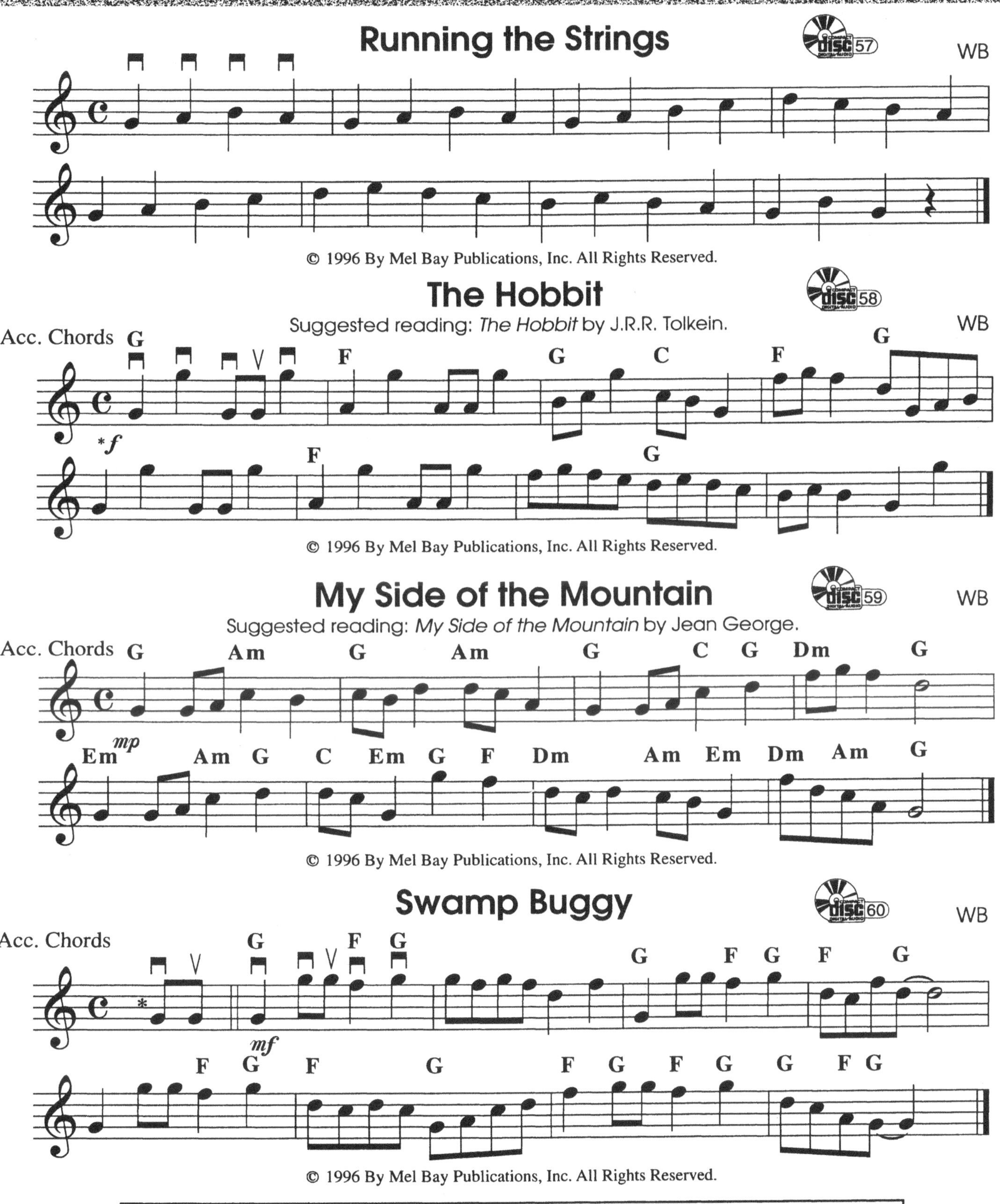

*** Pick-up notes are notes leading into the downbeat of the first measure of a song.**

**f forte - loud* *(see p. 131)*

Shadow of the Bull

Guitar Ensemble in Three Parts

Suggested reading: *Shadow of a Bull* by Wojciechowska

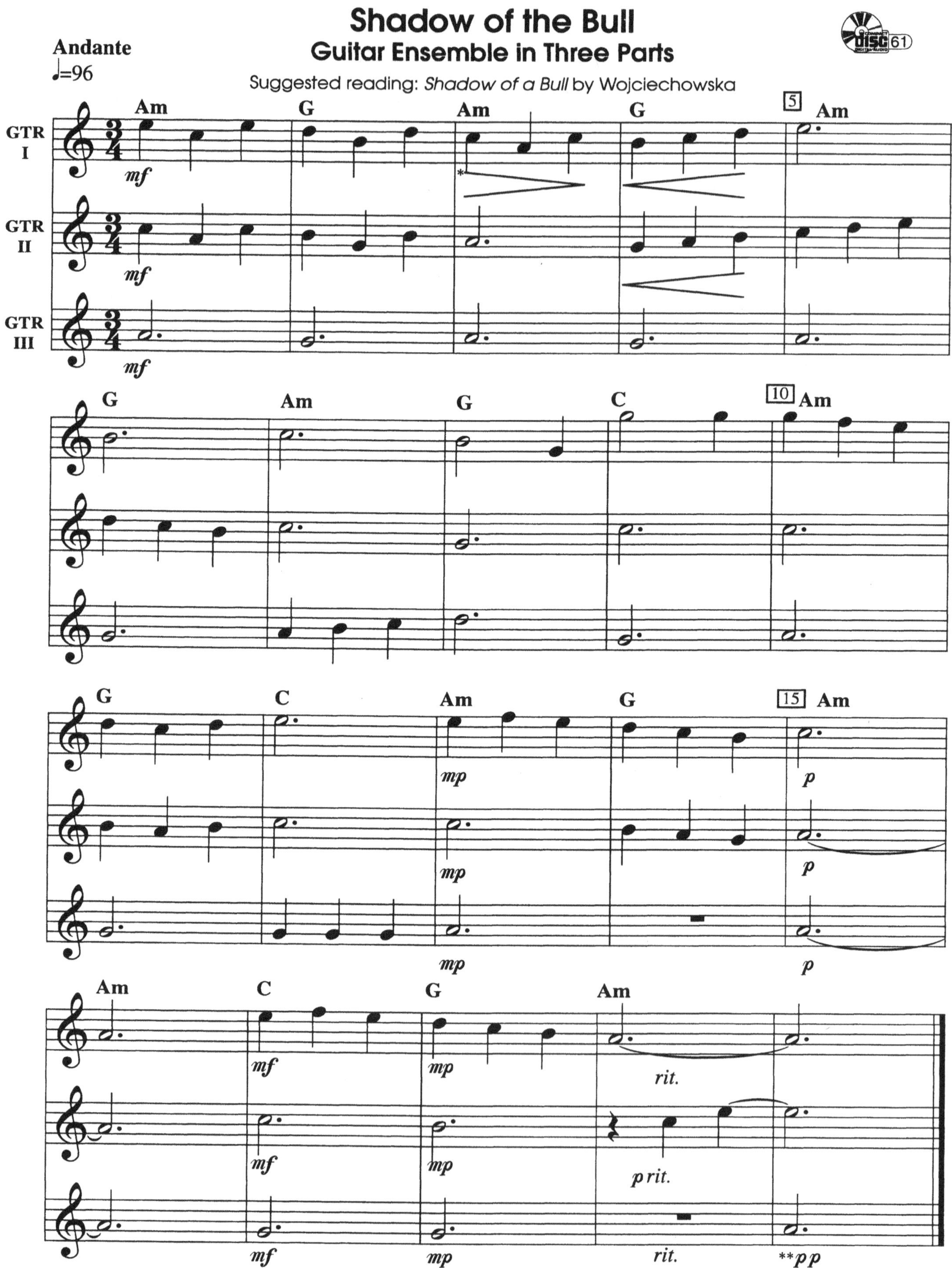

*de crescendo - gradually get softer

***pp* - very soft

New Strum Pattern

The pattern shown in the first measure works well with songs in 4/4 time. Remember to use the same strum pattern in every measure.

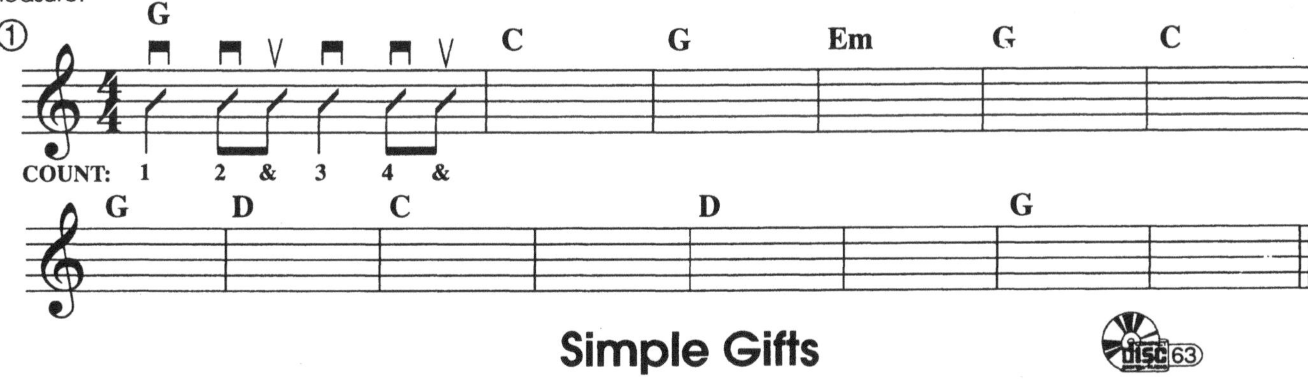

Simple Gifts

"Simple Gifts" is the most famous song of a historical American religious sect known as the Shakers. This song was used by American composer Aaron Copland as the theme of his ballet suite "Appalachian Spring." The Shakers began their sect in England in about 1706 but later, in 1774 under the leadership of Anne Lee, established a community in Watervliet, New York. The Shakers believed in a simple, communal lifestyle. All property was owned by the community. They invented the circular saw, cut nails, a washing machine, metal pen points and designed a style of furniture still popular today.

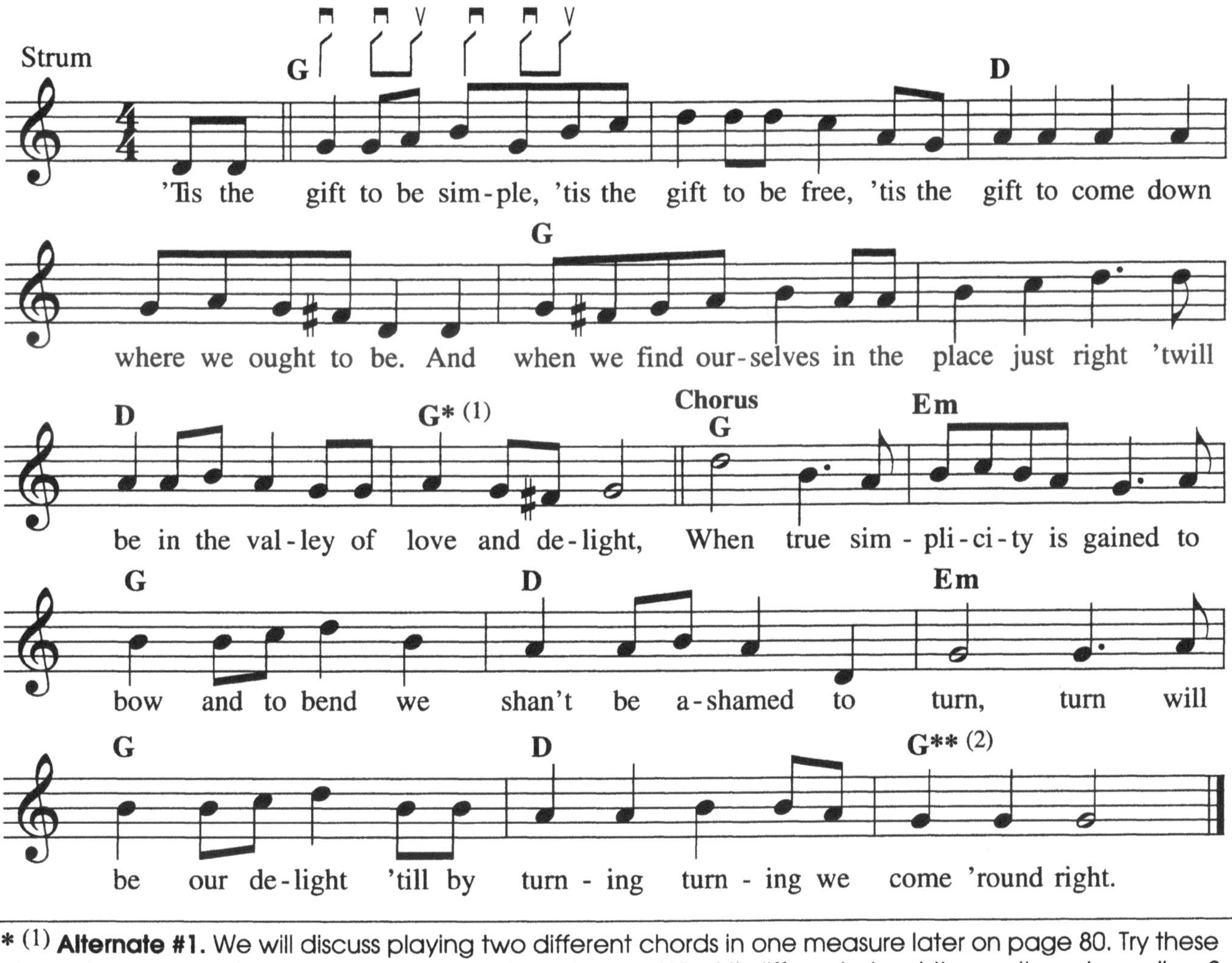

Strum

G D

'Tis the gift to be sim-ple, 'tis the gift to be free, 'tis the gift to come down

G

where we ought to be. And when we find our-selves in the place just right 'twill

D G* (1) Chorus G Em

be in the val-ley of love and de-light, When true sim - pli-ci-ty is gained to

G D Em

bow and to bend we shan't be a-shamed to turn, turn will

G D G** (2)

be our de-light 'till by turn - ing turn - ing we come 'round right.

* (1) **Alternate #1.** We will discuss playing two different chords in one measure later on page 80. Try these alternate measures to add color to the ending phrases. What is different about these alternate endings?

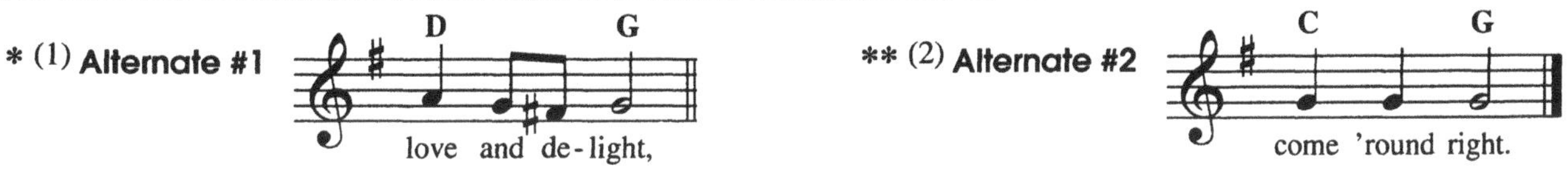

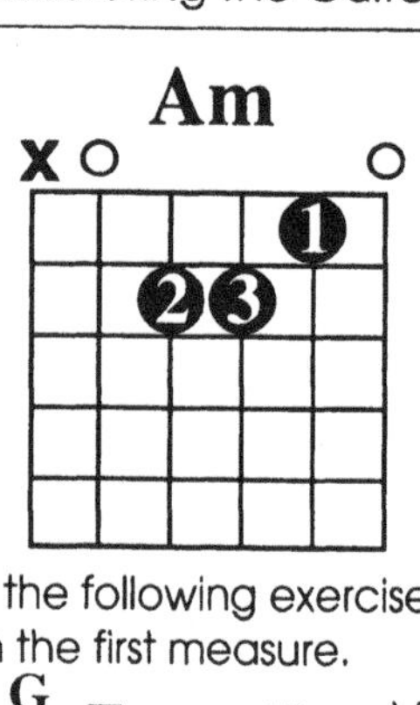

Learn the two new chords drawn here.

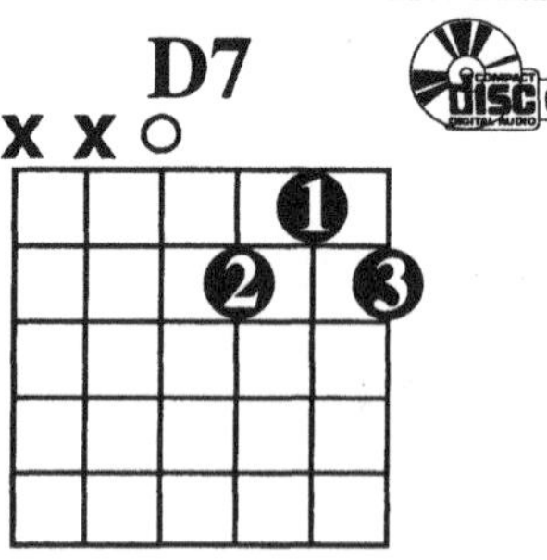

Practice the following exercises and songs which contain **Am** and **D7.** In each measure, play the strum pattern which is written in the first measure.

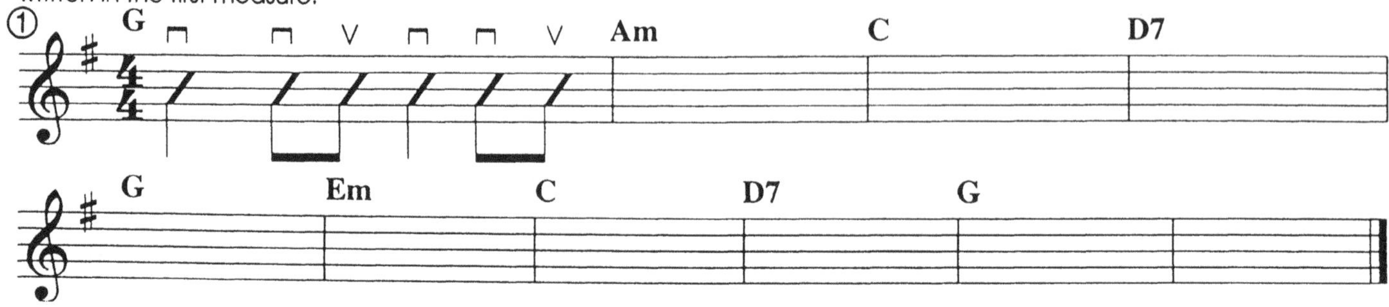

Molly Malone

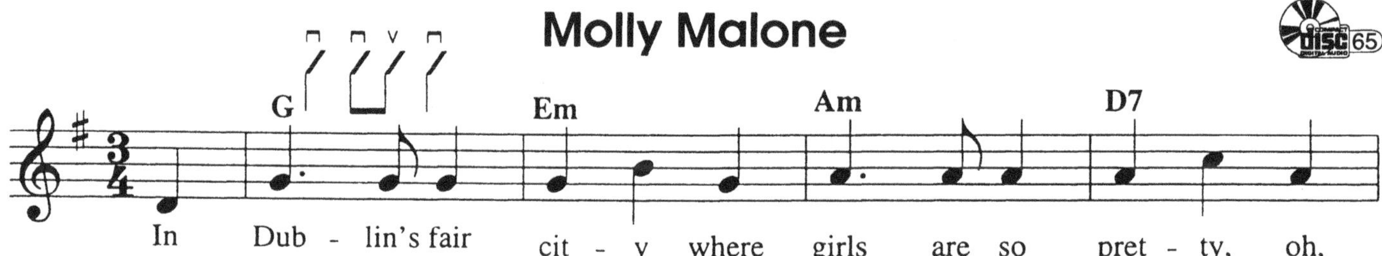

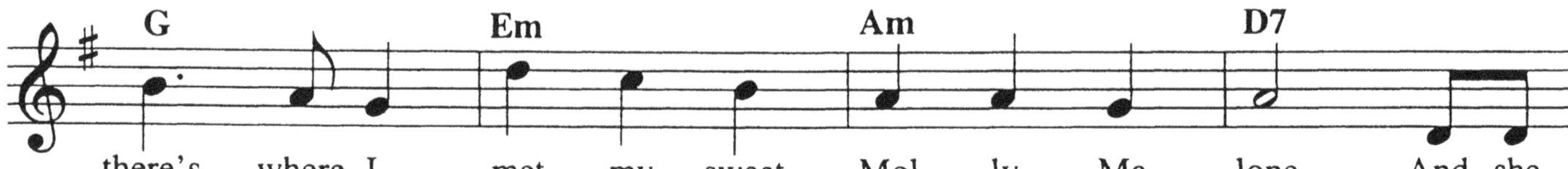

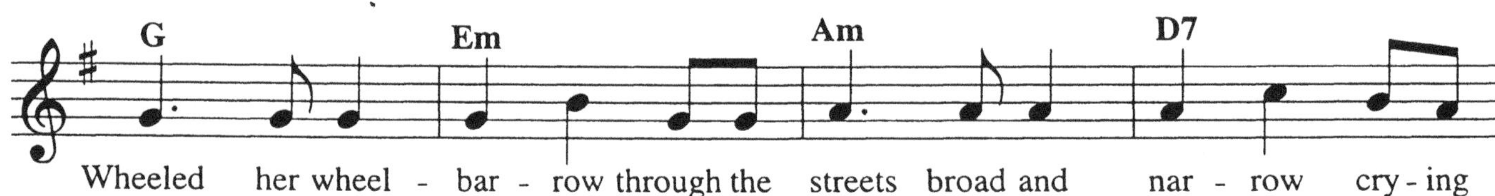

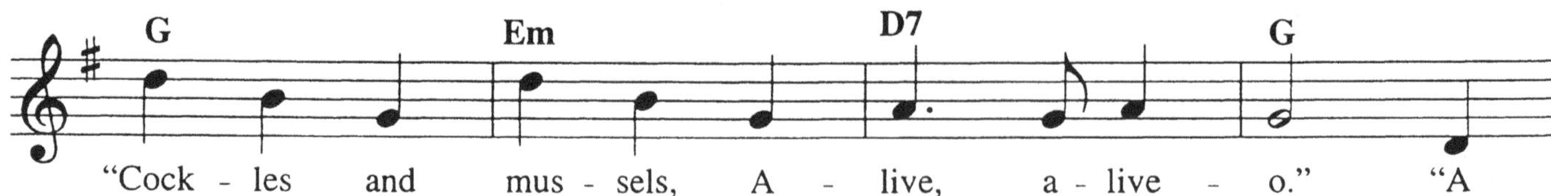

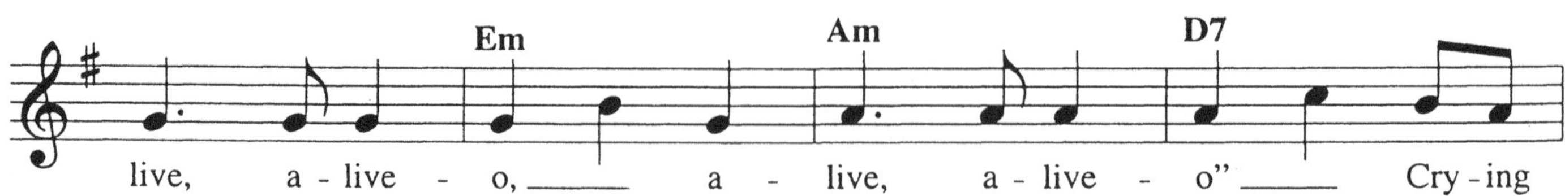

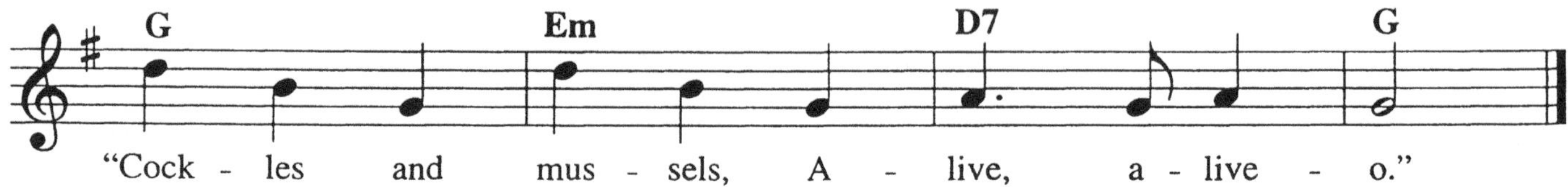

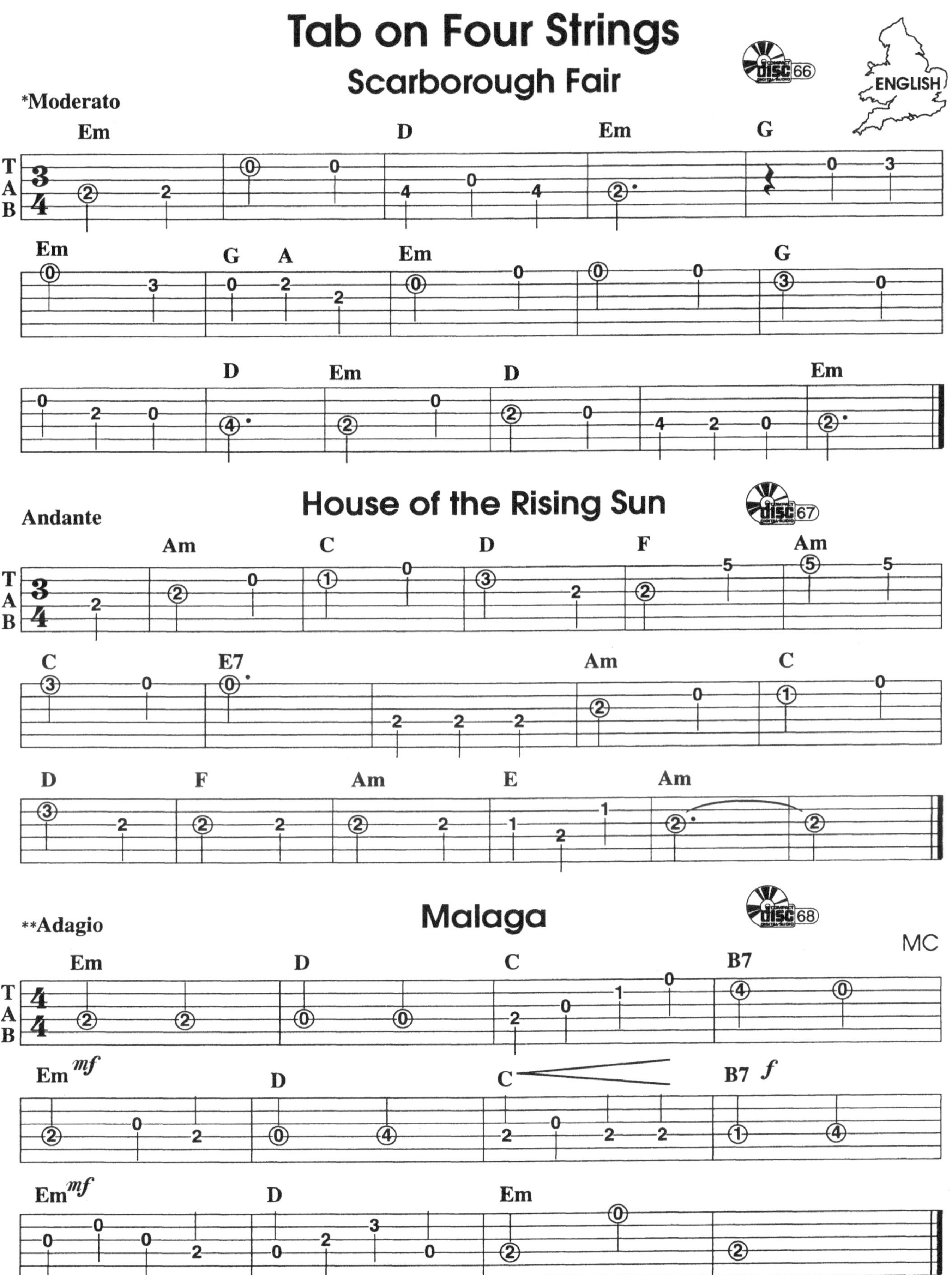

Moderato - medium speed
**Adagio - slowly*

Two More Strum Patterns in 4/4 Time

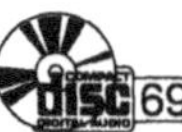

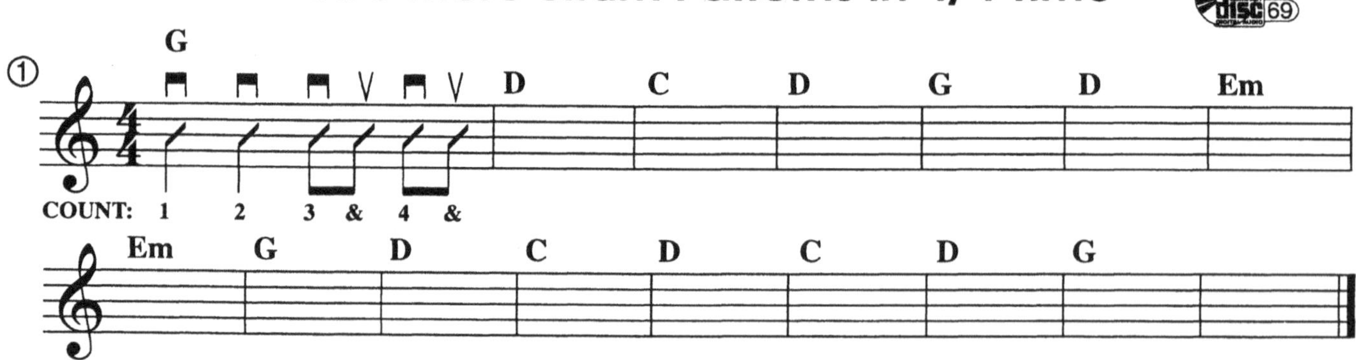

The Cruel War

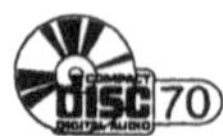

Suggested reading: *The Red Badge of Courage* by Stephen Crane (a story about the American Civil War.)

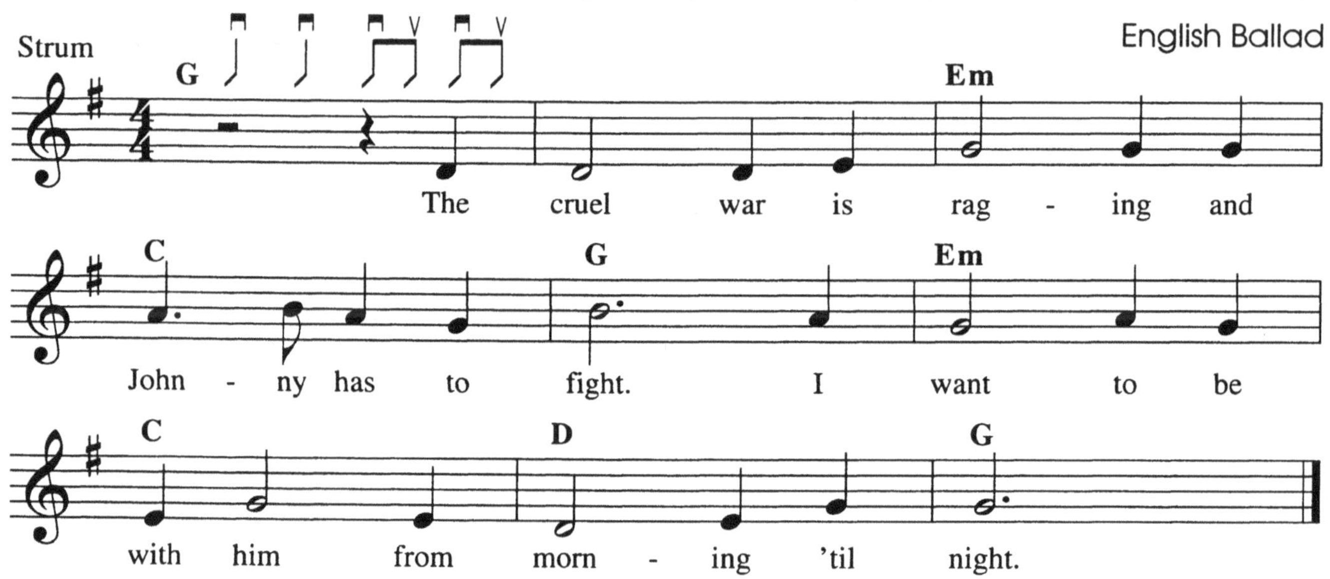

2. I'll go to your captain, get down upon my knees,
Ten thousand gold guineas, I'd give for your release.

3. Ten thousand gold guineas, it grieves my heart so;
Won't you let me go with you? Oh, no, my love, no.

4. Tomorrow is Sunday and Monday is the day,
Your captain calls for you, and you must obey.

5. Your captain calls for you, it grieves my heart so,
Won't you let me go with you? Oh, no, my love, no.

6. Your waist is too slender, your fingers are too small.
Your cheeks are too rosy to face the cannonball.

7. Your cheeks are too rosy, it grieves my heart so.
Won't you let me go with you? Oh, no, my love, no.

8. Johnny, oh Johnny, I think you are unkind.
I love you far better than all other mankind.

9. I love you far better than tongue can express,
Won't you let me go with you? Oh, yes, my love, yes.

10. I'll pull back my hair, men's clothes I'll put on,
I'll pass for your comrade as we march along.

11. I'll pass for your comrade and none will ever guess,
Won't you let me go with you? Yes, my love, yes.

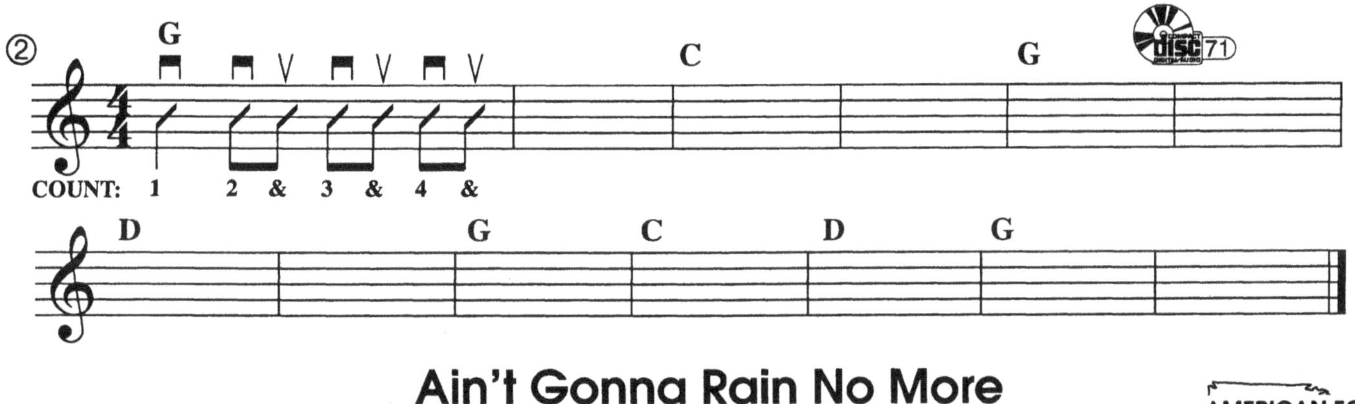

Ain't Gonna Rain No More

AMERICAN FOLK SONG

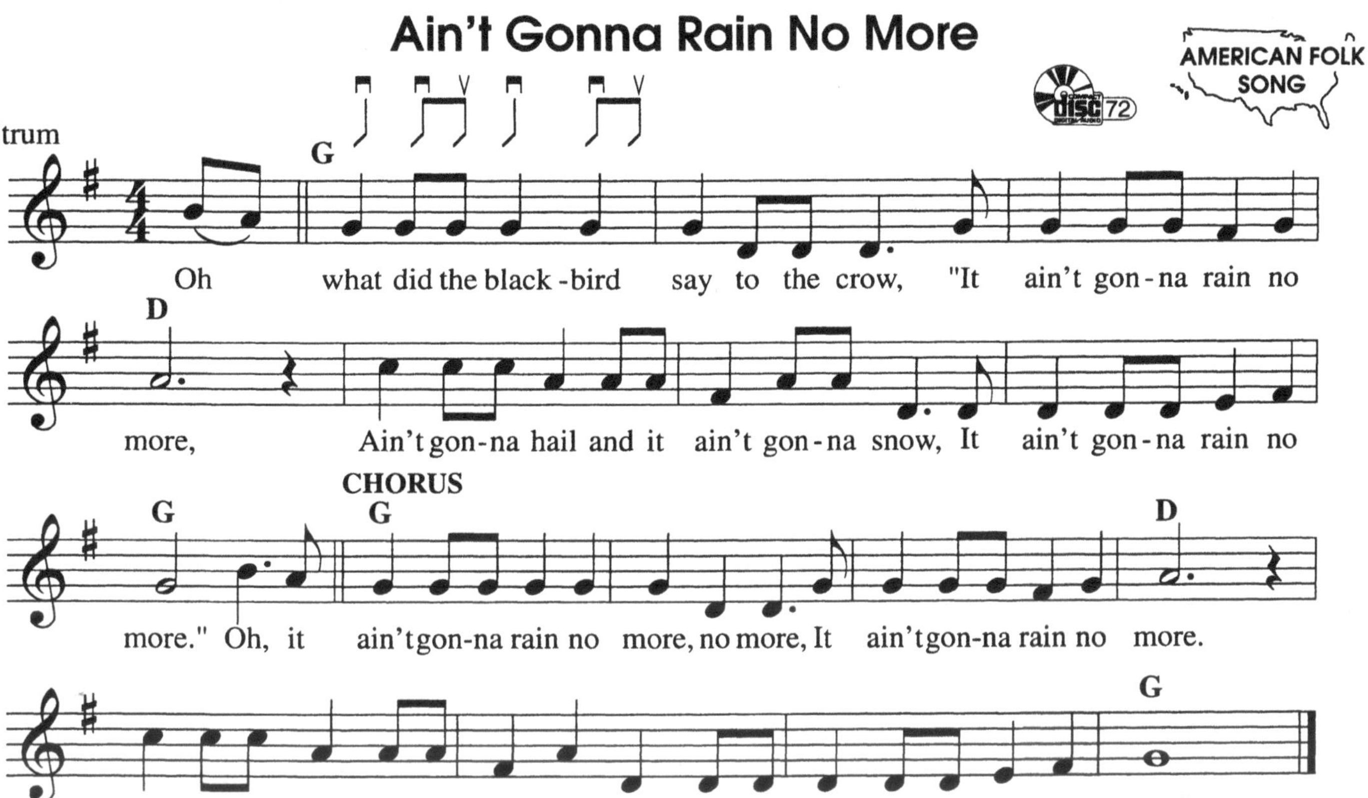

Verse 2:

G
Bake those biscuits good and brown,
D
It ain't gonna rain no more.
Swing your partner 'round and 'round,
G
It ain't gonna rain no more. *Chorus*

Verse 3:

G
It ain't gonna rain no more, no more,
D
It ain't gonna rain no more,
How do you suppose the old bird knows,
G
It ain't gonna rain no more. *Chorus*

Verse 4:

G
Thunder, lightning from the sky
D
It ain't gonna rain no more.
Saw Uncle Ezra floatin' by!
G
It ain't gonna rain no more? *Chorus*

Verse 5:

G
Pigs, cows, chickens and a goose!
D
It ain't gonna rain no more,
Whole darn barnyard's on the loose!
G
It ain't gonna rain no more! *Chorus*

Assignment: Make up your own verse to this song.

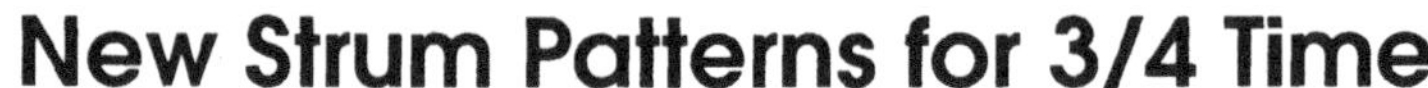

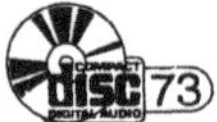

The following strum pattern will work well with songs written in 3/4 time.

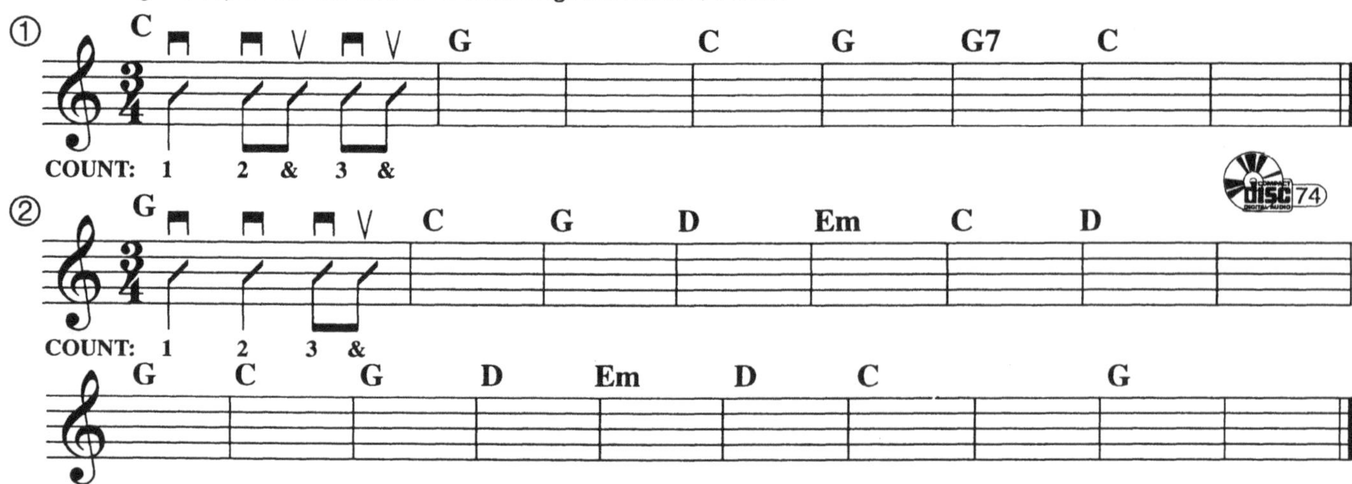

Play the following Mexican song using one of the strum patterns shown above.

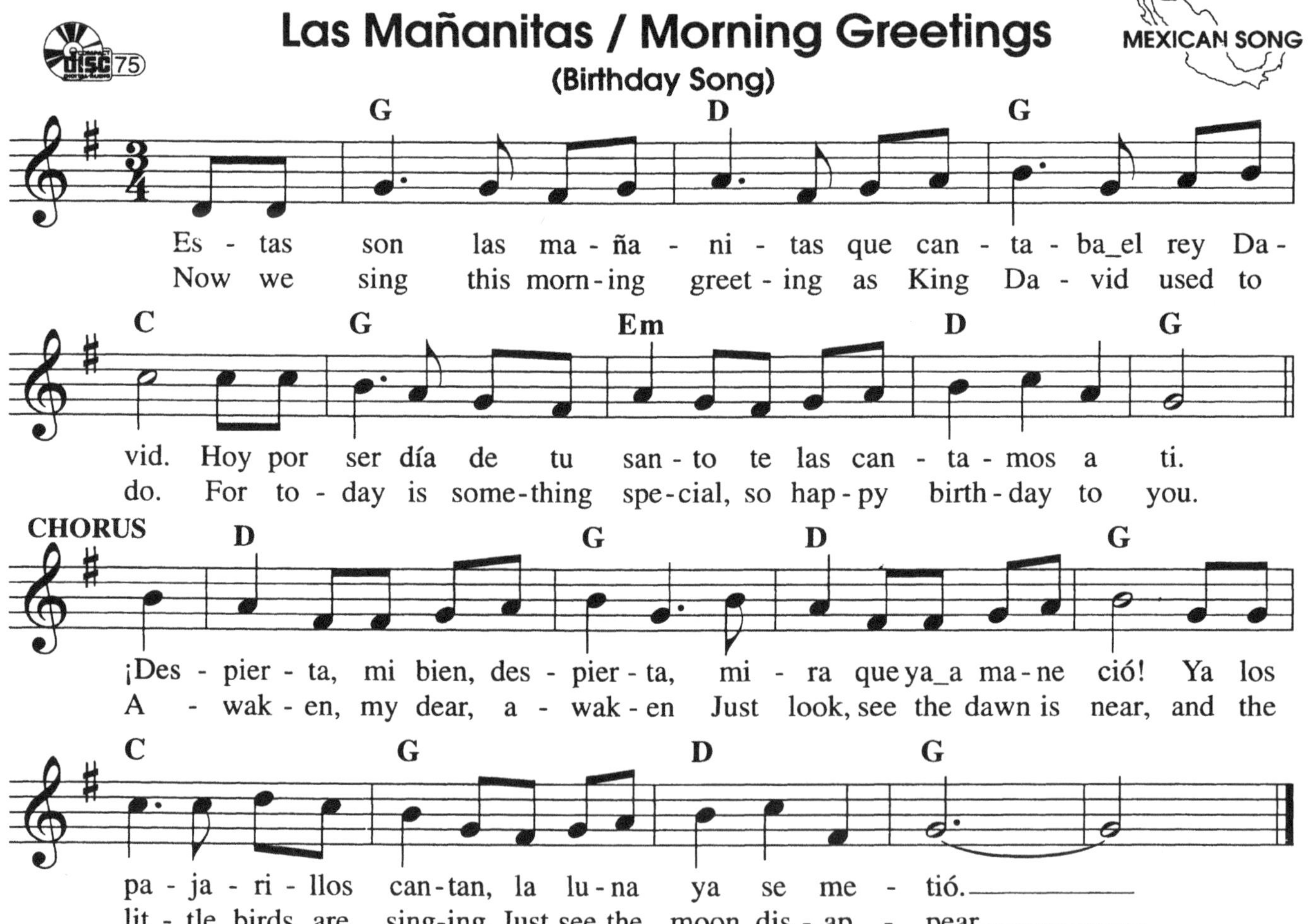

Si el sereno de la esquina
Me quisiera hacer favor,
De apagar su linternita
Mientras que pasa mi amor. *Chorus*

Amapolita morada
De los llanos de Tepic,
Si no estás enamorada,
Enamórate de mí. *Chorus*

Ahora sí señor sereno,
Le agradezco su favor;
Encienda su linternita,
Que ya ha pasado mi amor. *Chorus*

Oh lamplighter on the corner,
Please just listen to my song,
And blow out your little lantern
As my love passes along. *Chorus*

Little poppy, scarlet poppy,
On the meadows growing free,
If you're not in love with someone,
Please fall in love then with me. *Chorus*

Oh lamplighter, I do thank you
For the favor that you've done.
Now you can relight your lantern,
Because my love's come and gone. *Chorus*

Blues

Blues is an American music form. Its earliest forms were work songs and "field hollers" sung among the slaves. At first, blues was strictly a vocal music form, but gradually musicians of all types embraced the form. Traditional blues has 12 measures. Blues songs reflect times of troubles but often have a humorous twist.

Around 1900 a black band leader named W.C. Handy became popular and wrote such hits as "St. Louis Blues," "Beale Street Blues" and "Memphis Blues." Other early Blues artists included Blind Blake, Robert Johnson, Lonnie Johnson, and Louis Armstrong. Later band leaders like Count Basie and Duke Ellington, along with singers like Billie Holiday and Jimmy Rushing furthered the form. The modern blues era was ushered in by saxophonist Charlie Parker. Today blues is an essential part of all jazz and popular music. Who are some of today's famous blues' artists?

Midnight Special

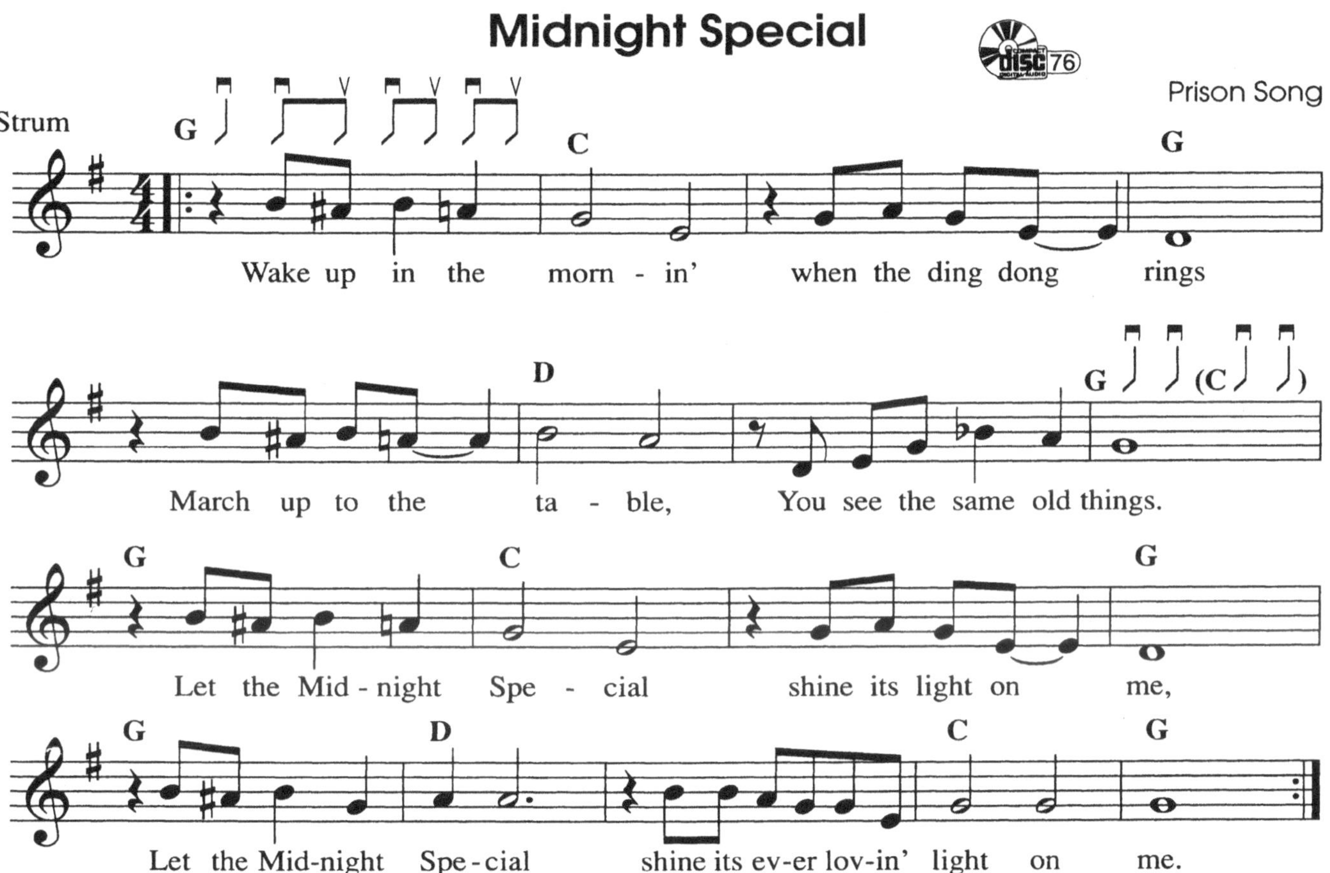

Verse 1. Sister Sadie said she loved me, But she told a lie (G, C, G)
'Cause she has not seen me- since last July. (D, G)
She brought me coffee, she brought me tea, (C, G)
She brought me lots of things, but not the jail house key. (D, C, G) *Chorus*

Thought Question: What is the Midnight Special?

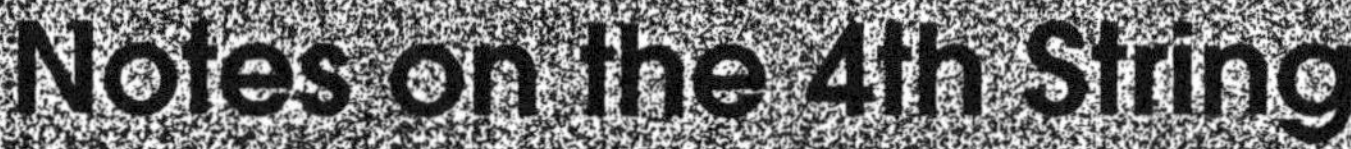

Notes on the 4th String

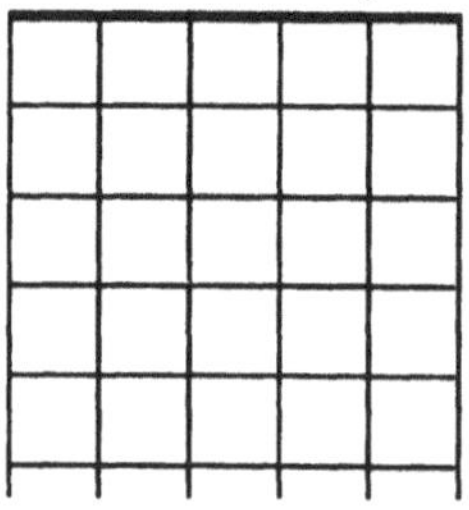

D

D is the 4th string - open

T
A 0
B

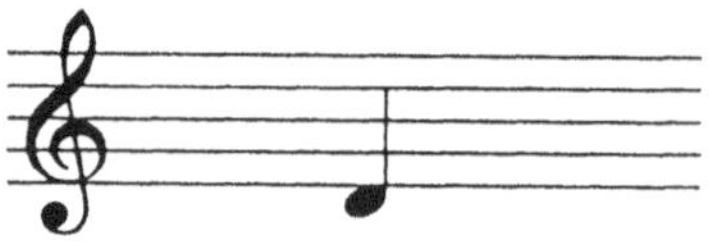

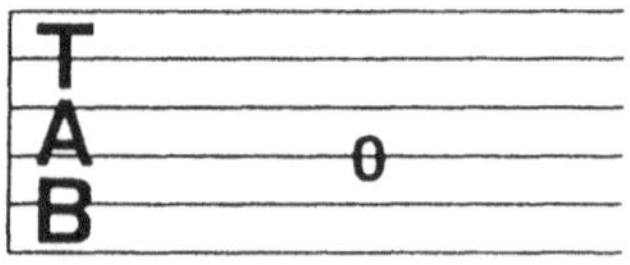

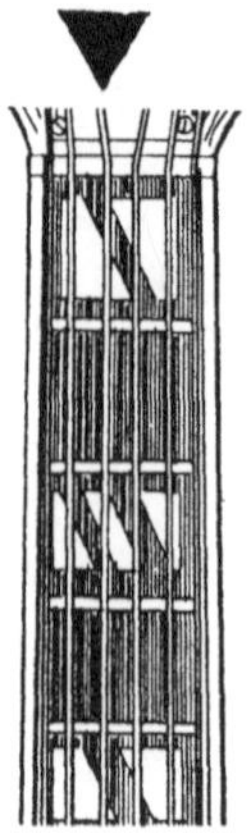

D is the 4th string, open.

Play D

disc 77

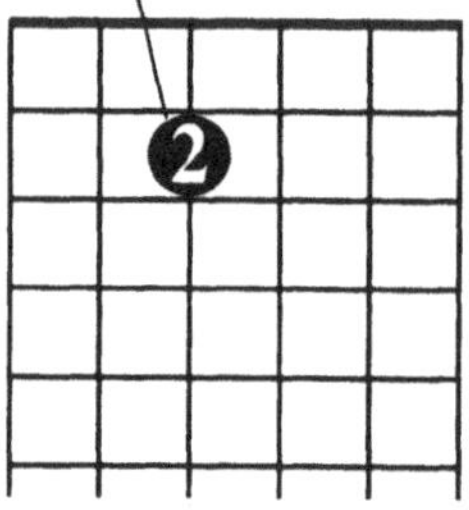

E

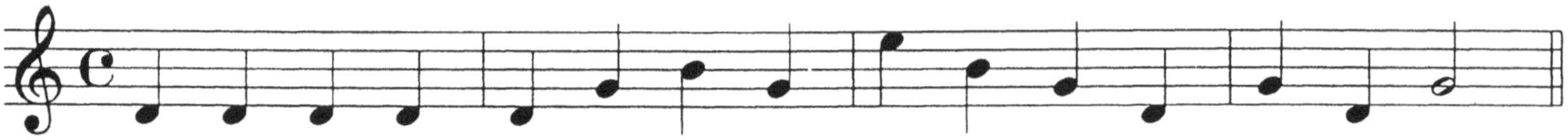

E is 2nd finger - 2nd fret - 4th string

T
A 2
B

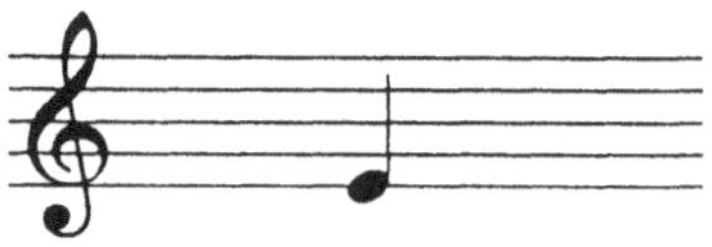

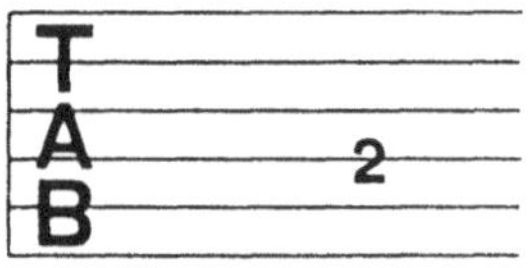

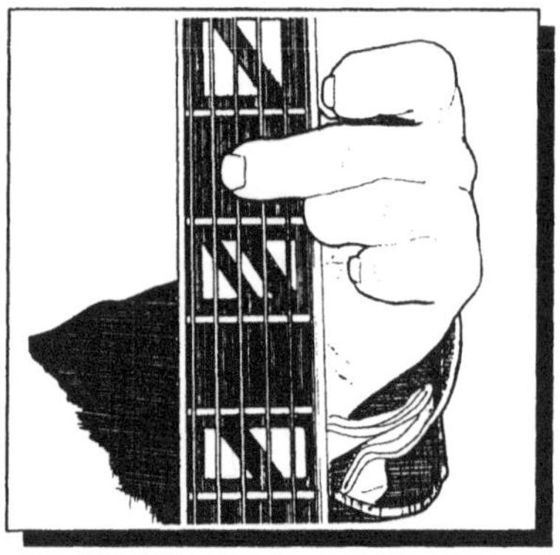

E is 2nd finger, 2nd fret, 4th string.

D - E

disc 78

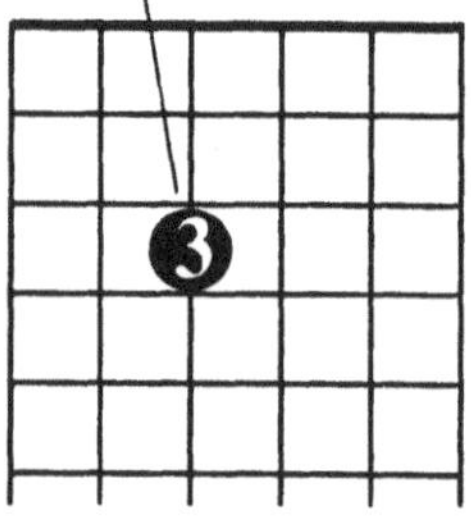

F

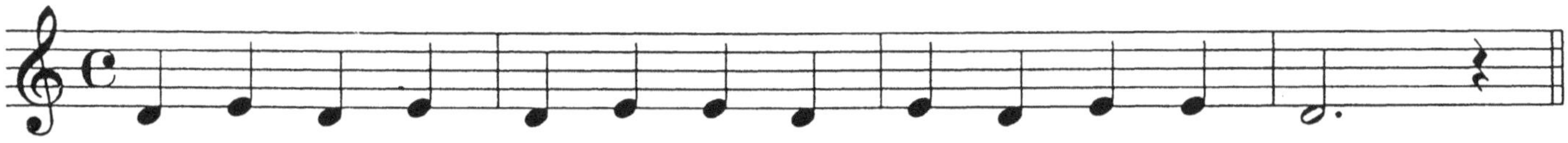

F is 3rd finger - 3rd fret - 4th string

T
A 3
B

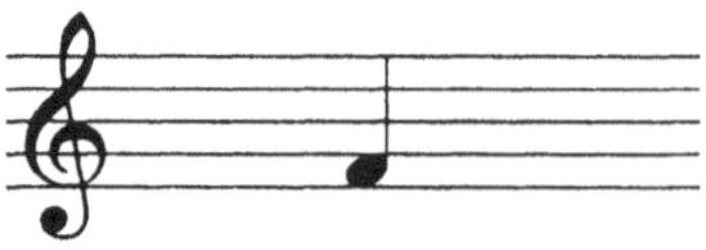

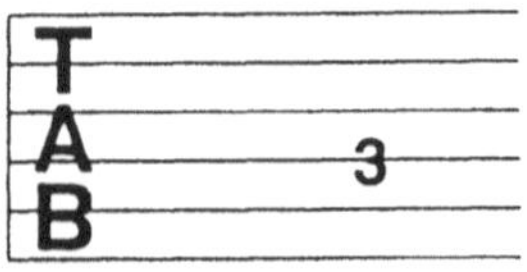

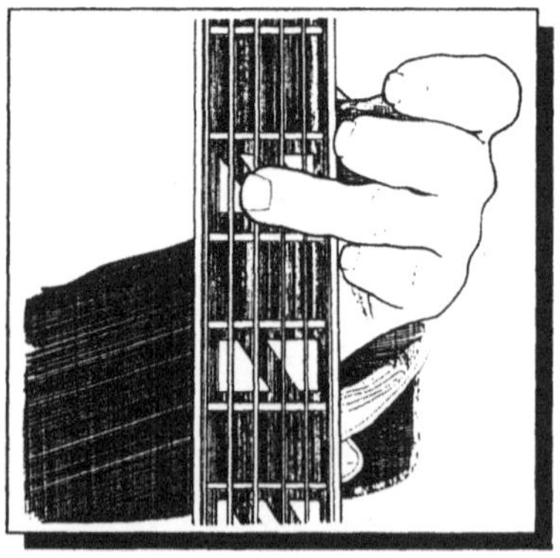

F is 3rd finger, 3rd fret, 4th string.

D - E - F

disc 79

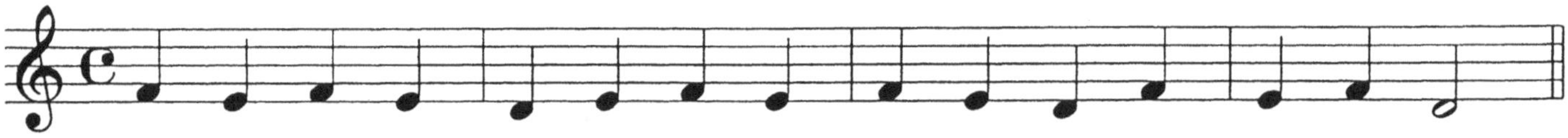

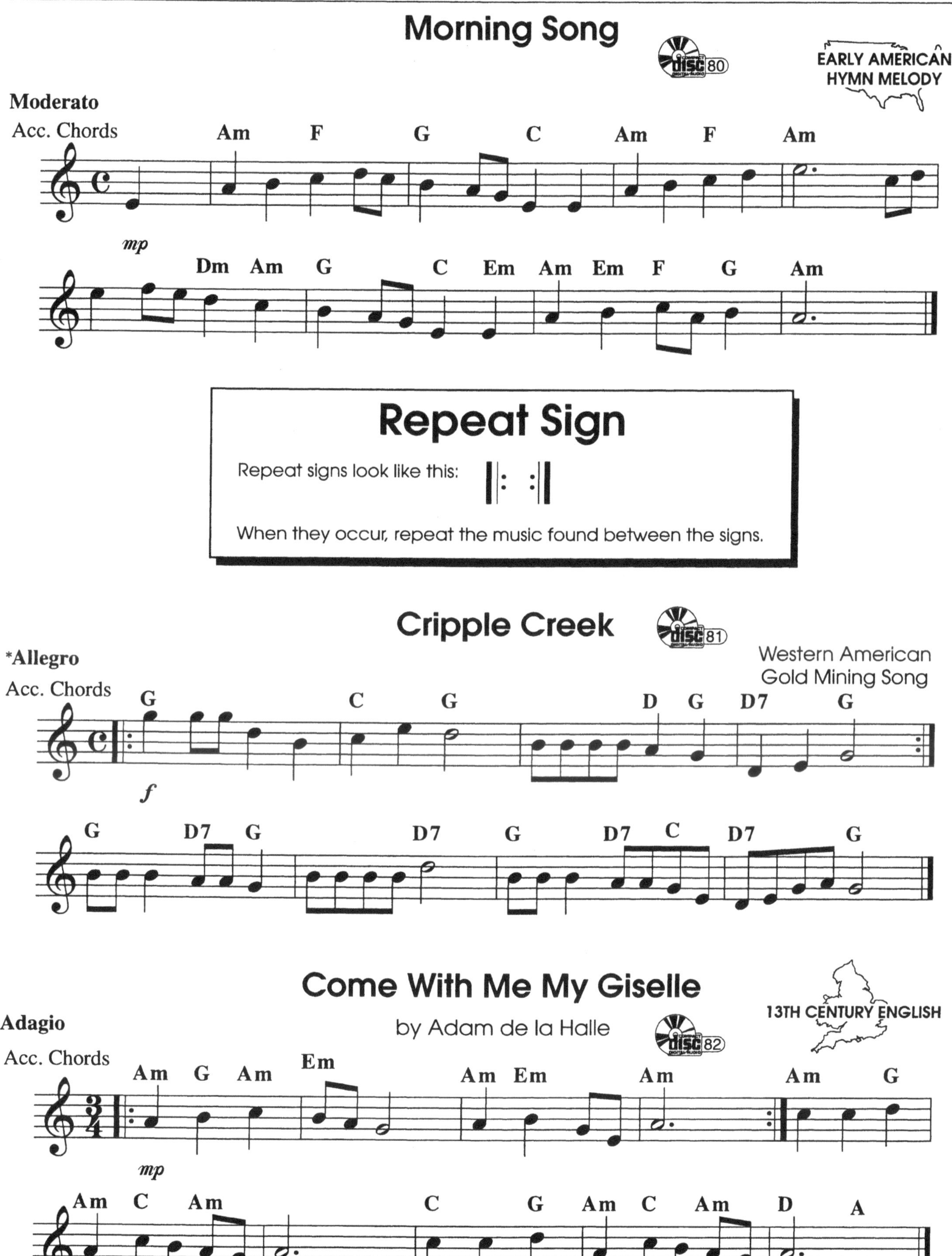

*Allegro - quickly (see p. 131)

A7 and E7 Chords

The fingerings for **A7** and **E7** chords are shown on the diagrams below. Notice there are two fingerings for each chord. One is not necessarily better than the other and either fingering may be used. The first forms are easier. Eventually, both forms of each chord should be learned.

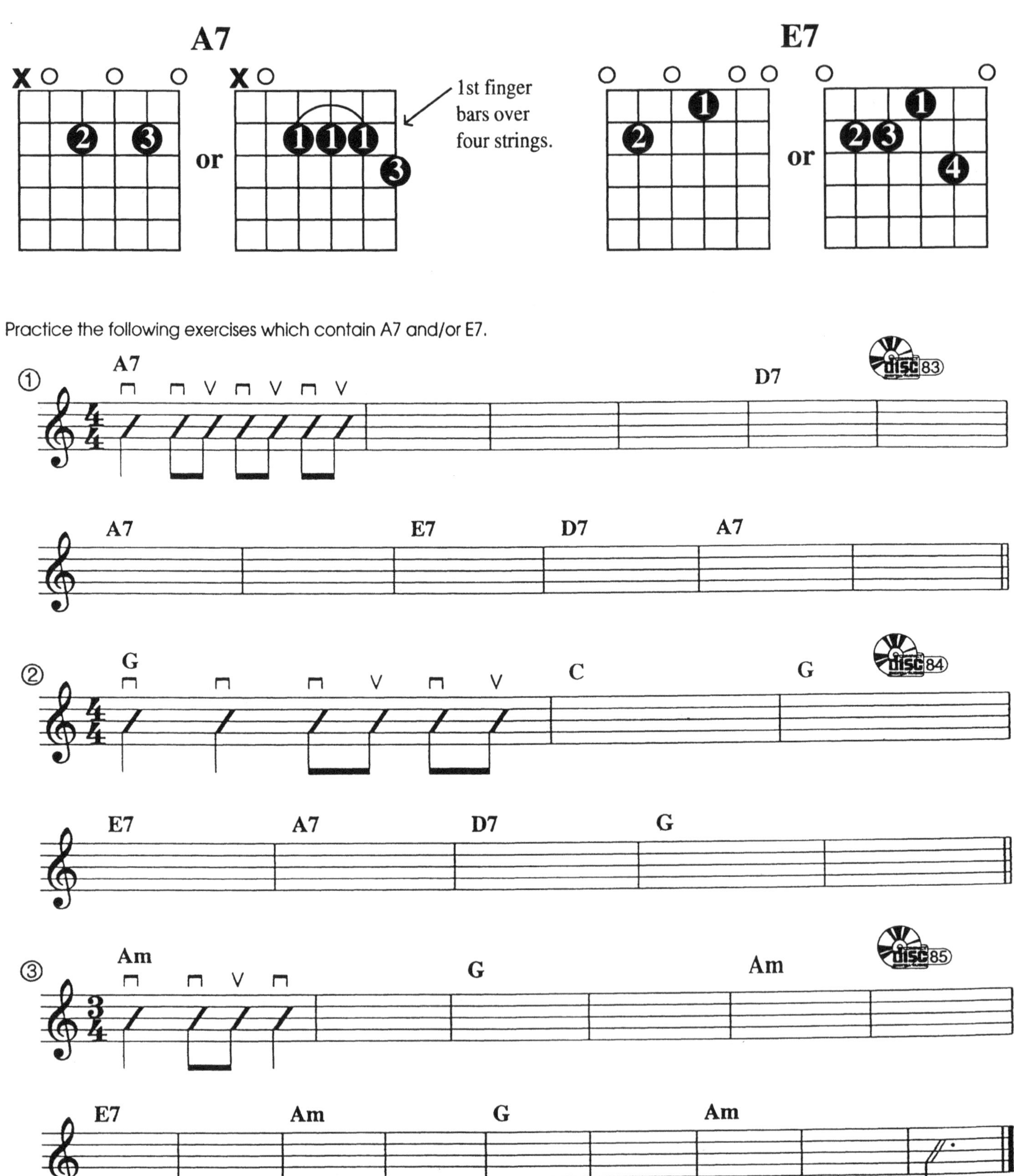

Practice the following exercises which contain A7 and/or E7.

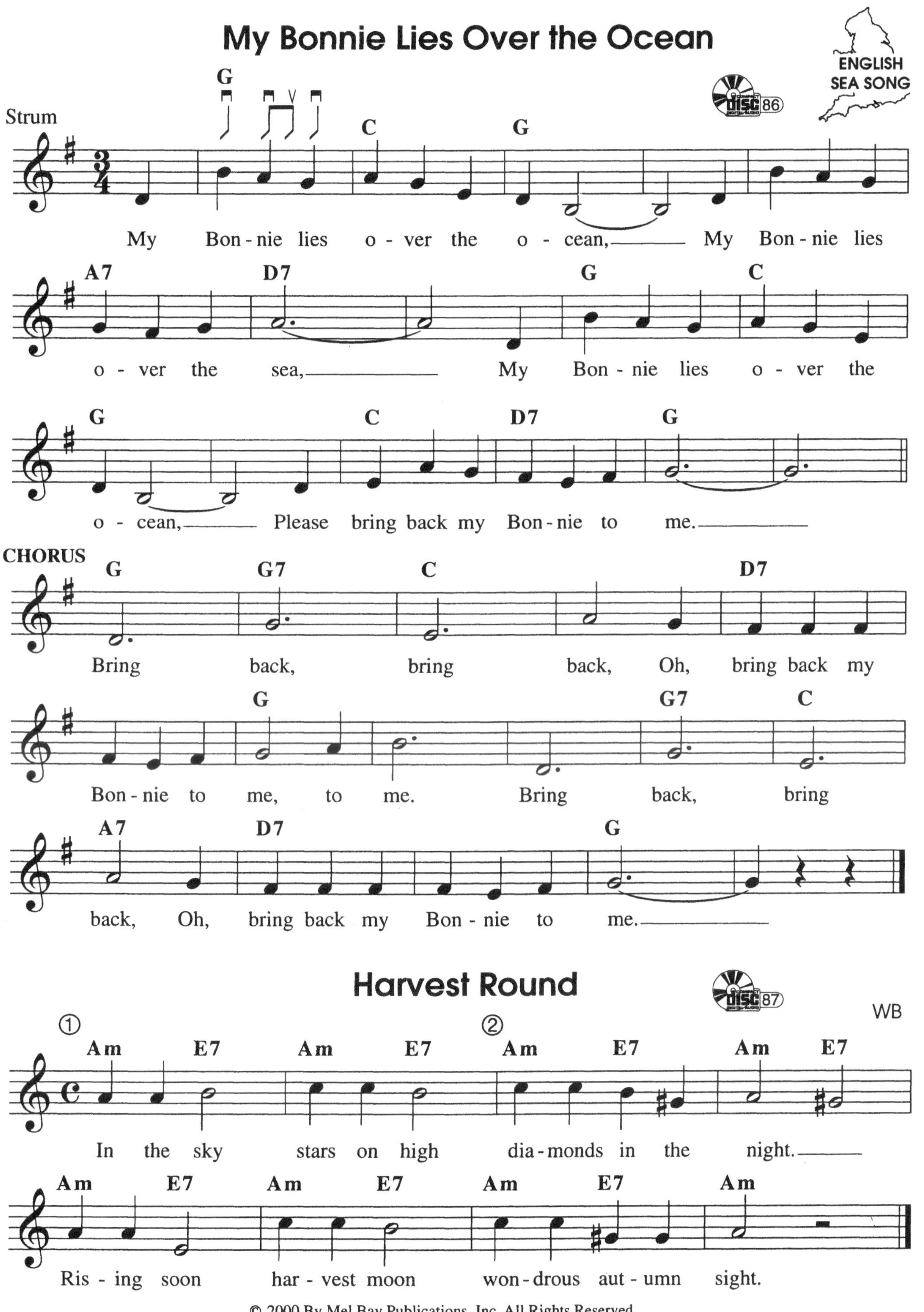
My Bonnie Lies Over the Ocean
ENGLISH SEA SONG
86
Strum
G C G
My Bon-nie lies o-ver the o-cean, My Bon-nie lies
A7 D7 G C
o-ver the sea, My Bon-nie lies o-ver the
G C D7 G
o-cean, Please bring back my Bon-nie to me.
CHORUS
G G7 C D7
Bring back, bring back, Oh, bring back my
G G7 C
Bon-nie to me, to me. Bring back, bring
A7 D7 G
back, Oh, bring back my Bon-nie to me.
Harvest Round
87
WB
①
②
Am E7 Am E7 Am E7 Am E7
In the sky stars on high dia-monds in the night.
Am E7 Am E7 Am E7 Am
Ris-ing soon har-vest moon won-drous aut-umn sight.

B7 and Bm Chords

Learn the **B7** and **Bm** chords drawn below and practice the exercises containing these chords. As with the other exercises in this book, use the same strum pattern which is written in the first measure to play the other measures.

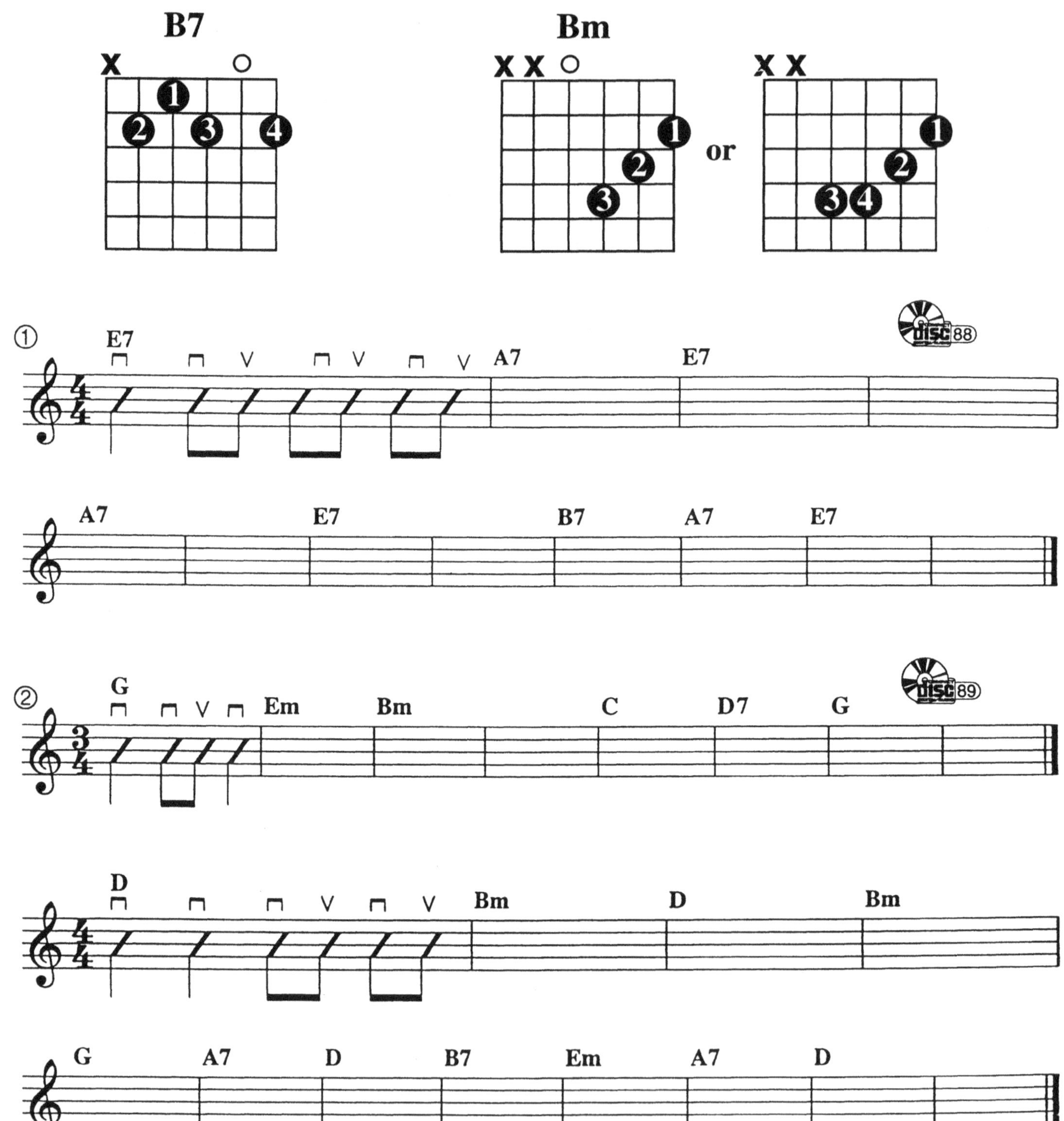

Land of the Silver Birch

Canadian Indian

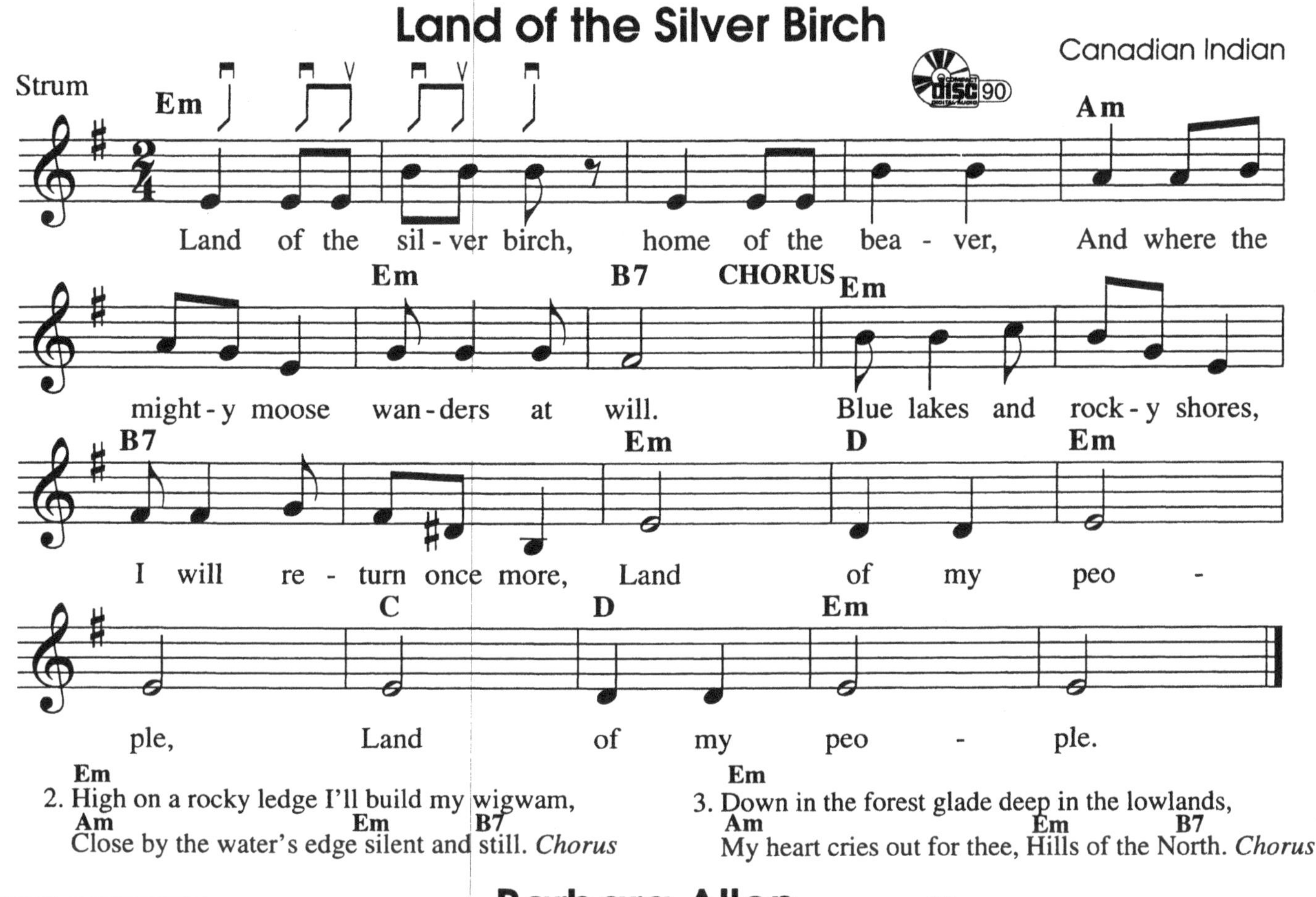

2. High on a rocky ledge I'll build my wigwam,
Close by the water's edge silent and still. *Chorus*

3. Down in the forest glade deep in the lowlands,
My heart cries out for thee, Hills of the North. *Chorus*

Barbara Allen

Vocabulary: aspen, corpse, briar.

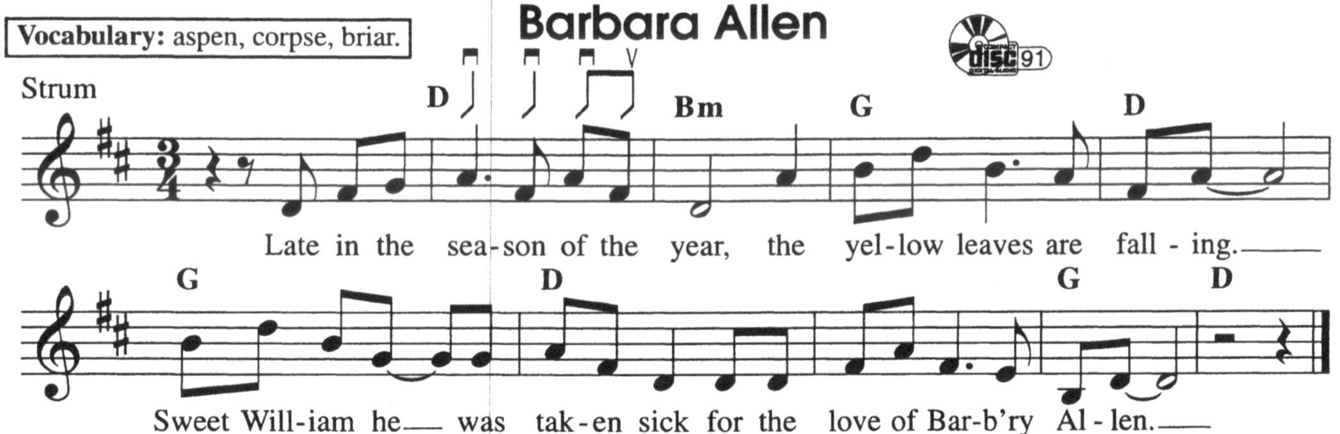

2. He sent his servant to the town,
The town where she was dwelling.
Rise you up to your master's call
If your name be Barbara Al-len.

3. 'Twas in the merry month of May.
When green buds, they were swellin',
Sweet William on his deathbed lay
For the love of Barb'ry Allen

4. He sent his servant to the town
Where Barb'ry was a dwellin',
"My master's sick and bids you come,
If your name be Barb'ry Allen."

5. So slowly, slowly got she up,
And slowly she came nigh him,
And all she said when she got there,
"Young man, I think your dyin'."

6. "Oh, yes, I'm sick and very sick,
For death is in me dwellin'.
No better can I ever be,
If can't have Barb'ry Allen."

7. Then lightly tripped she down the stairs,
He trembled like an aspen,
"'Tis vain, 'tis vain, my dear young man,
To pine for Barb'ry Allen."

8. He turned his pale face to the wall,
For death was in him dwellin',
"Adieu, adieu, my friends all 'round,
Be kind to Barb'ry Allen."

9. As she went down the long piney walk,
The birds, they kept a-singin',
They sang so clear, they seemed to say,
"Hard-hearted Barb'ry Allen."

10. She looked to the east, she looked to the west,
She spied his corpse a-comin',
"Lay down, lay down that deathly frame
That I may look upon him."

11. The more she looked, the more she wept
Till she burst out a-crying;
"Oh take from me this very young man,
I think that I am dying."

12. They took him to the new churchyard,
And that is where they laid him.
They buried his lover by his side,
Her name-was Barbara Allen.

13. Out of his grave there sprang a rose,
And our of hers a briar
They grew and tied a true lover's knot,
The rose around the briar.

The Blues Progression

One of the most popular forms of the blues is the 12-bar blues progression. The term ***progression*** refers to a series of chords. ***Twelve-bar*** means the progression is 12 measures long. *The three chords used in the basic 12-bar progression are the I, IV, and V chords,* The **I chord** (sometimes called the **tonic**) has the same letter name as the key in which you are playing. For example, the I chord in the key of C is C. The **IV chord (subdominant)** has the letter name which is four steps up the major scale from the I chord. The IV chord in the key of C is F. The **V chord (dominant)** has the same letter name as the fifth step up the major scale from the I chord. The V chord in the key of C is G. The following chart shows the I, IV, and V chords in the different keys. The most popular guitar keys are shown below. In the blues 7th chords are frequently used.

I (Tonic)	IV (Subdominant)	V (Dominant)
E (7)	A (7)	B (7)
A (7)	D (7)	E (7)
D (7)	G (7)	A (7)
G (7)	C (7)	D (7)

The formula for building the basic 12-bar blues progression is: four measures of the I chord, two measures of the IV chord, two measures of the I chord, one measure of the V chord, one measure of the IV chord, and two measures of the I chord. It's very common to replace the last measure of the I chord with a V chord if the progression is going to be repeated. This last measure is sometimes called the ***turnaround.*** The advantage of knowing the Roman numeral formula is that, by plugging in the correct I, IV, and V chords, you can play the blues in any key.

The following exercise is the basic 12-bar blues progression, Notice that the number of measures that each chord is played fits the blues formula. The chords in parentheses are the chords which would be used to play the blues in the key of E. Seventh chords (7) are commonly used on every chord in the blues because of their dissonant quality.

Play the following progression strumming down four times in each measure. While it may seem overly simple, strumming down four times in a measure was, and is, a fairly popular technique. Accent beats two and four.

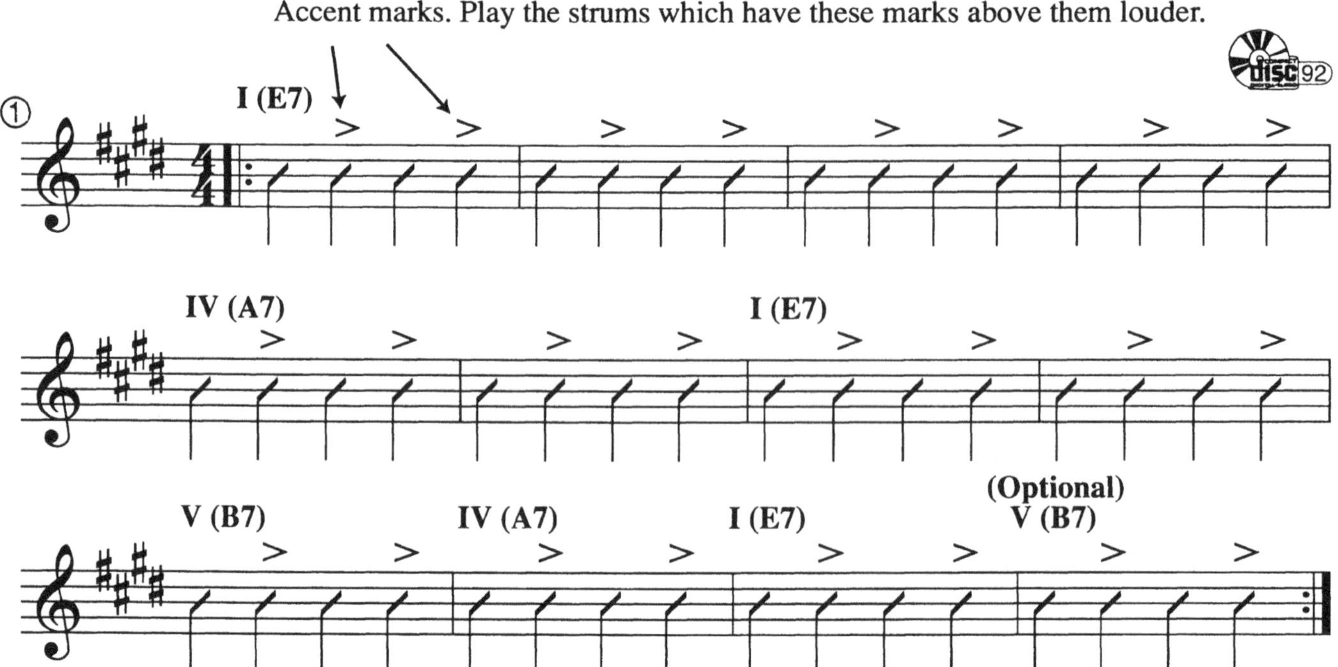

The next progression is a very **common variation of the 12-bar blues**. The IV chord has been added in the second measure. Remember, the V chord in the last measure is optional. This chord can be played if the progression is going to be repeated. When not repeating the progression, play the I chord in the last measure. Practice strumming this exercise. In each measure of the progression, play the strum pattern which is written in the first measure, This strum pattern works well when playing songs in 4/4.

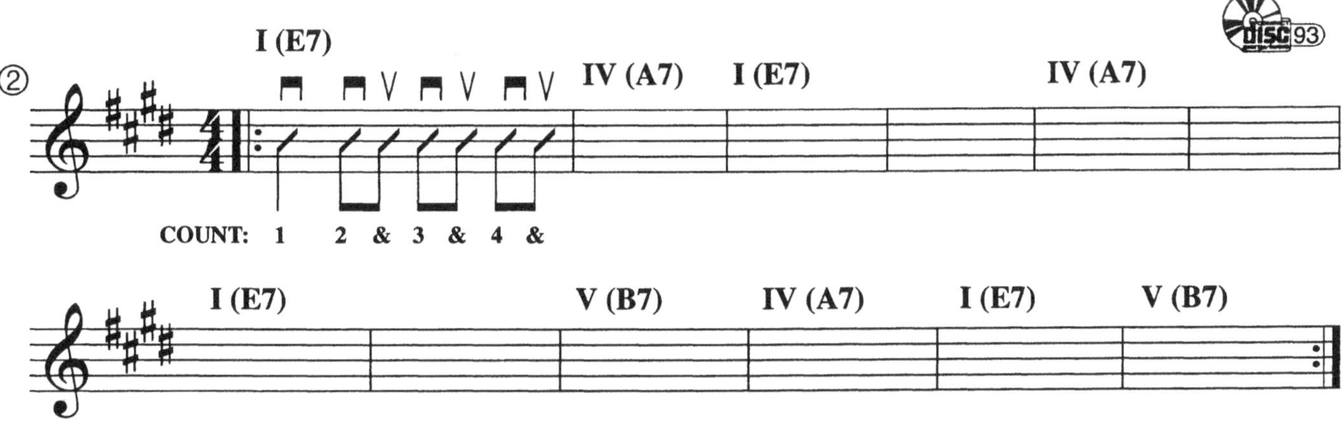

Strum the next progression which is a **blues in the key of A**. In each measure, use the strum pattern which is written in the first measure. This is another strum pattern which works to accompany songs in 4/4.

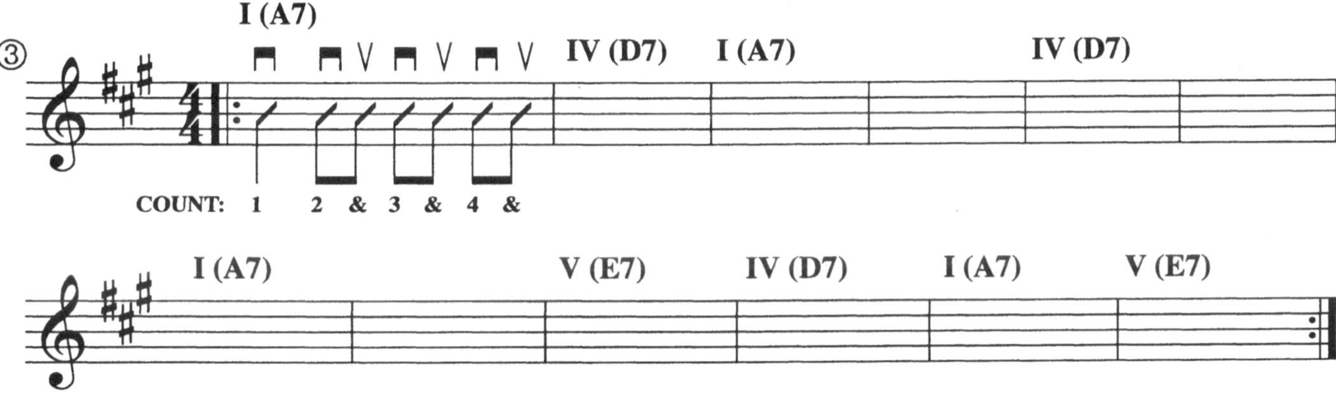

To play the blues in a minor key, the i and iv chords are minor and the V chord is still a seventh chord. Small Roman numerals indicate minor chords. Practice strumming the following blues in A minor. Use any of the strum patterns for 4/4. Remember to use the same strum pattern in each measure,

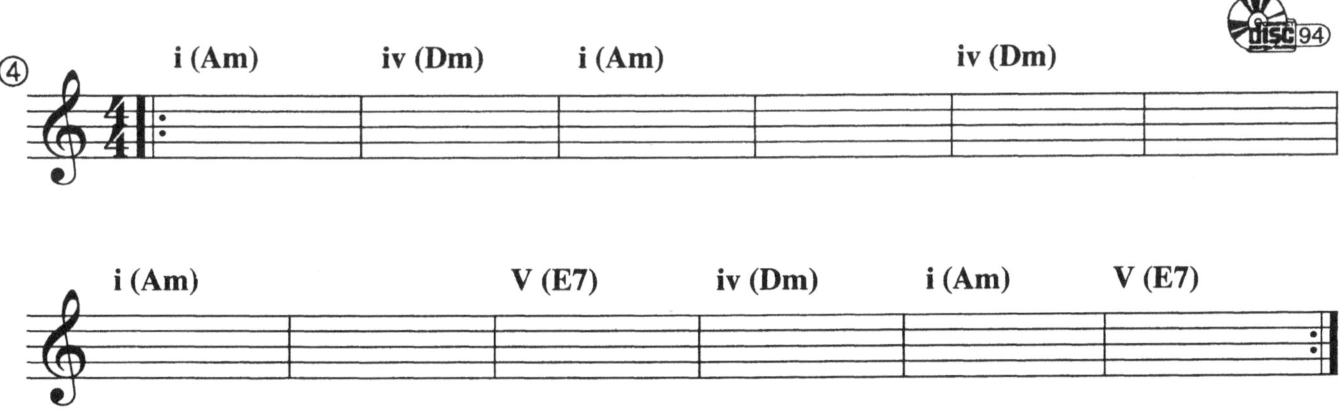

Practice strumming the following **blues songs**. Notice each song uses the 12-bar blues progression.

Baby Don't Love Me

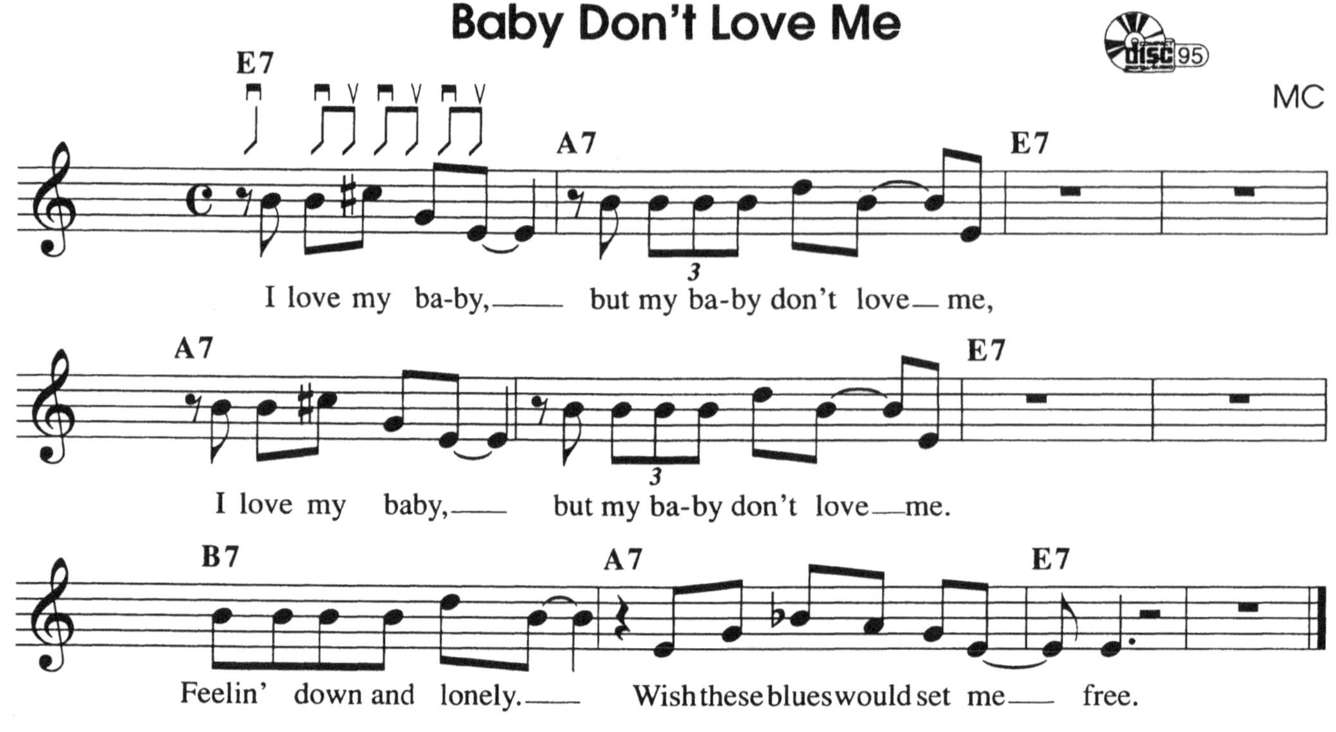

Writing Blues Lyrics

Writing lyrics to a blues song can be very simple. All that is required is to rhyme one word. The common blues progression is twelve measures long. This 12-measure progression can be divided into three groups of four measures. Each group of four measures is called a ***phrase***. Phrases are separated by pauses in the melody.

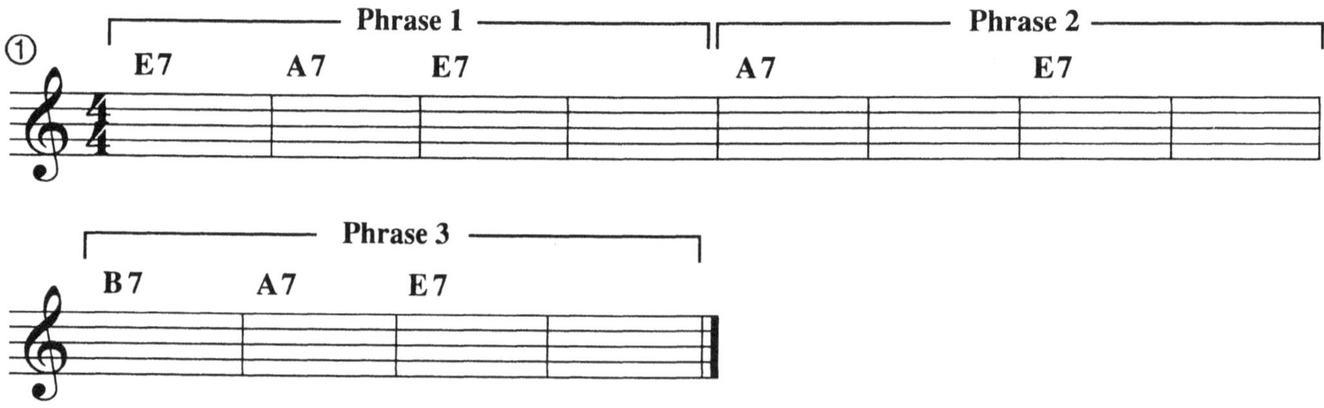

After each phrase there is usually a pause. Within each phrase, one or two sentences of lyrics can be written. For example:

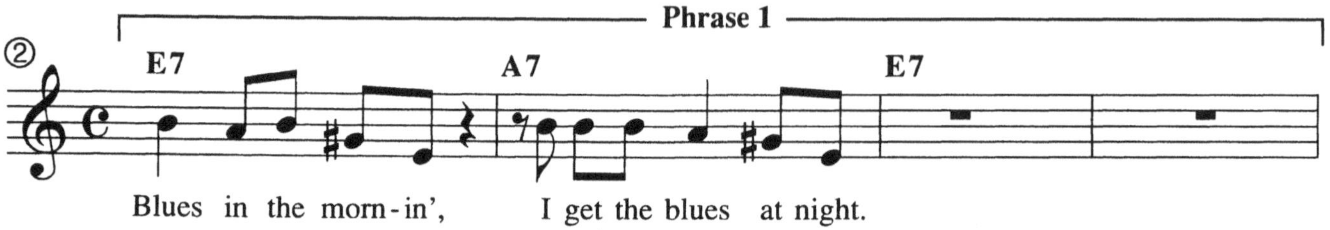

In the blues, it is very common for the lyrics and the melody in the second phrase to be the same as the lyrics and melody in the first phrase.

③
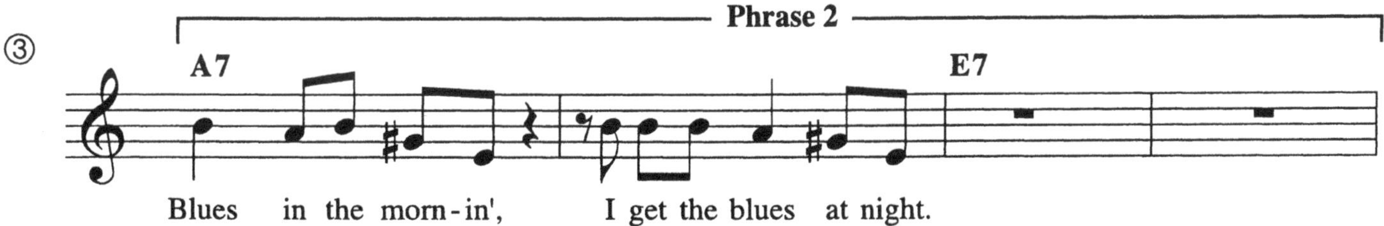

In the third phrase the lyrics and the melody usually change and the last word of the third phrase rhymes with the last word in phrases 1 and 2.

④
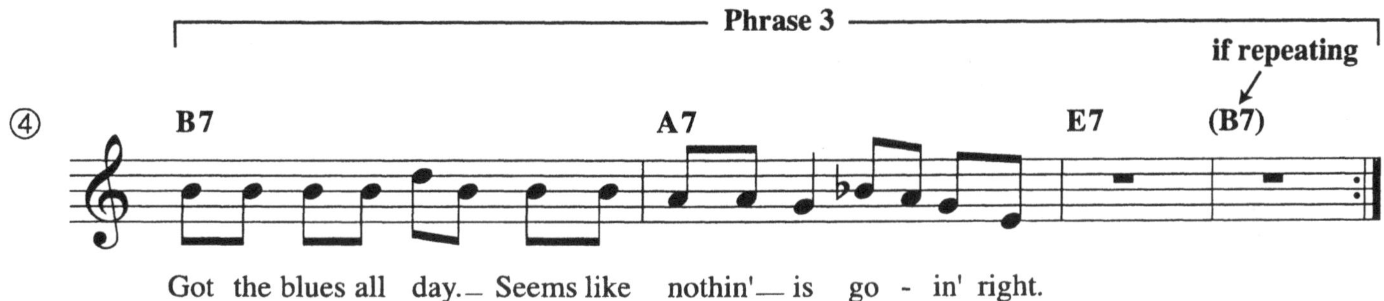

Written below is a 12-bar blues melody. Write in your own lyrics under the notes. You may have to modify the rhythm of the melody slightly to fit your words.

⑤
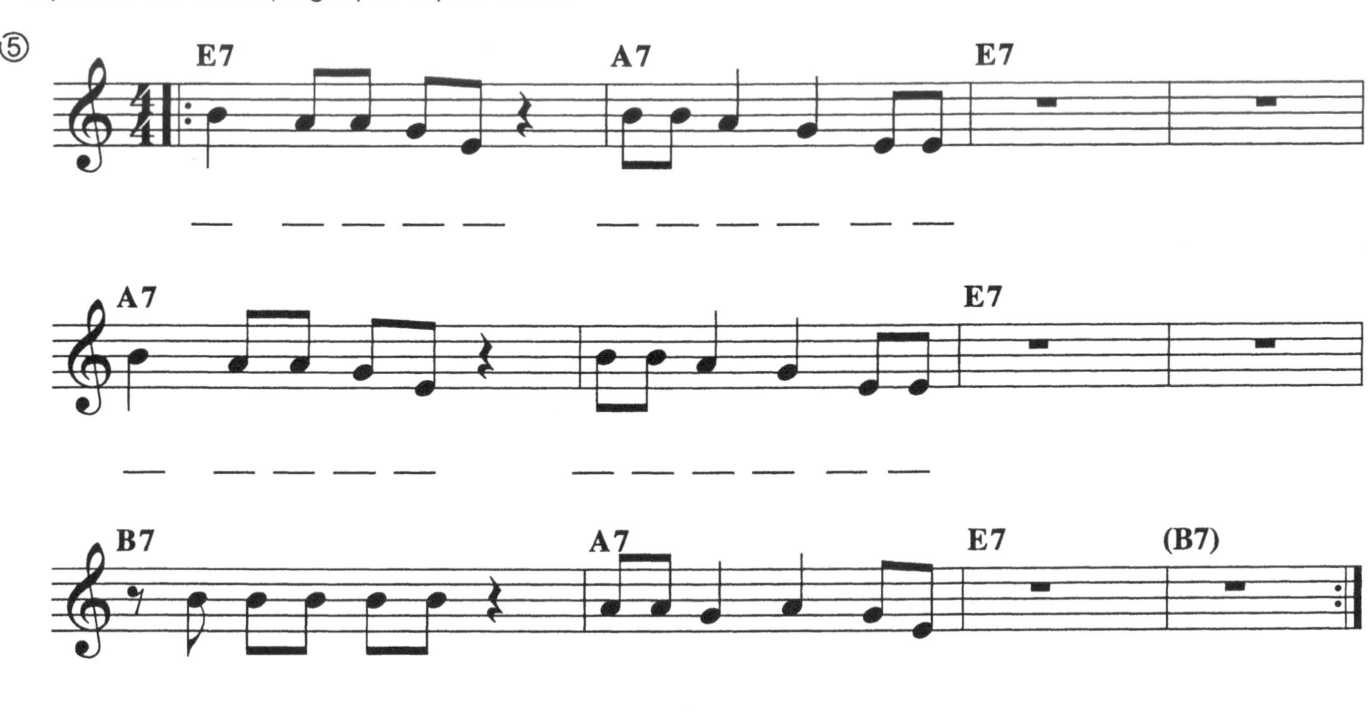

Syncopation

Syncopation means placing the accent on a beat (or a part of the beat) which is normally weak. Syncopation is often done by playing a note on the up beat (second half of the beat, or the "*and*") and letting that note ring through the first half of the next beat. Syncopated rhythms are commonly written as a quarter note or quarter notes between two eighth notes. Sometimes the second eighth note is replaced by a dot after the quarter note. The following illustrations show how syncopated rhythms are written out and how they are counted. Some of the songs, exercises, and solos in this book contain these rhythms. It's important that you understand how they are counted. Hold any note and practice tapping your foot on the beat while you play and count the rhythms written below.

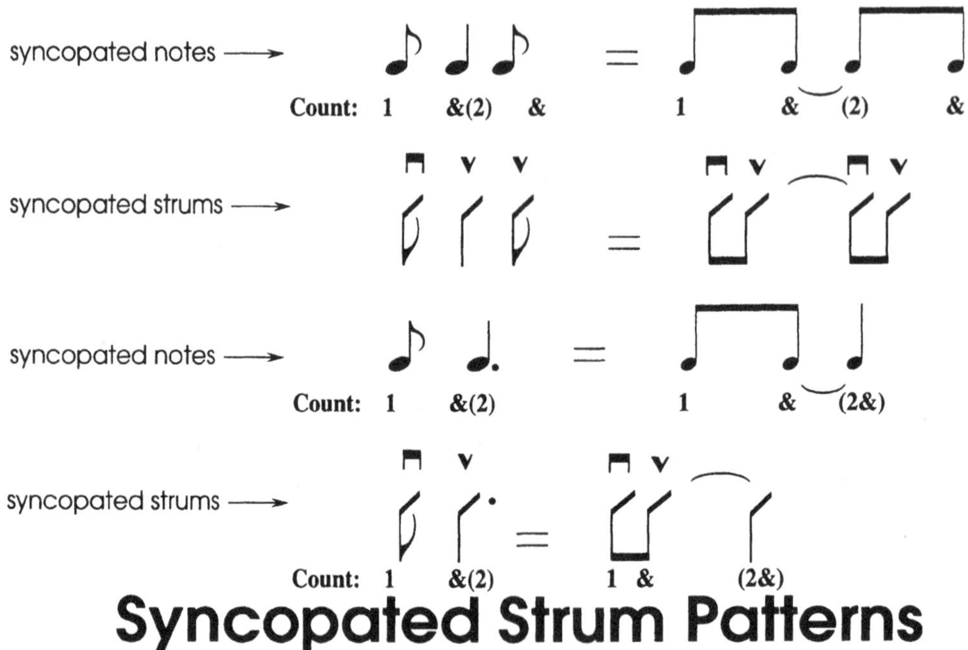

Syncopated Strum Patterns

Shown below are common strum patterns for 4/4 and 3/4 which contain syncopation. They can be used to play the chords to any song in 4/4 or 3/4. Each pattern takes one measure to complete. Hold any chord and practice each pattern. Count aloud as you play the patterns. Be sure to wait for the tied strums.

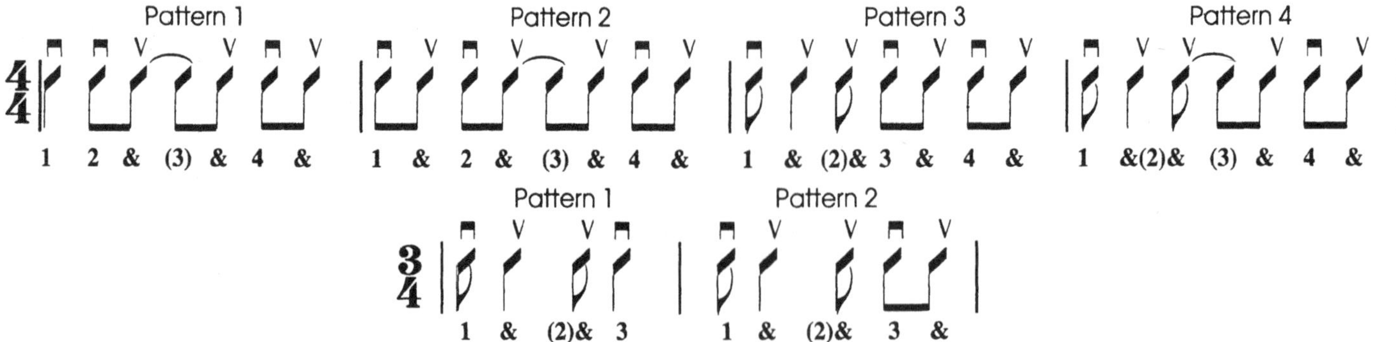

Practice the following exercises which contain **syncopated strums.** Use the pattern which is written in the first measure to play each measure of the exercise.

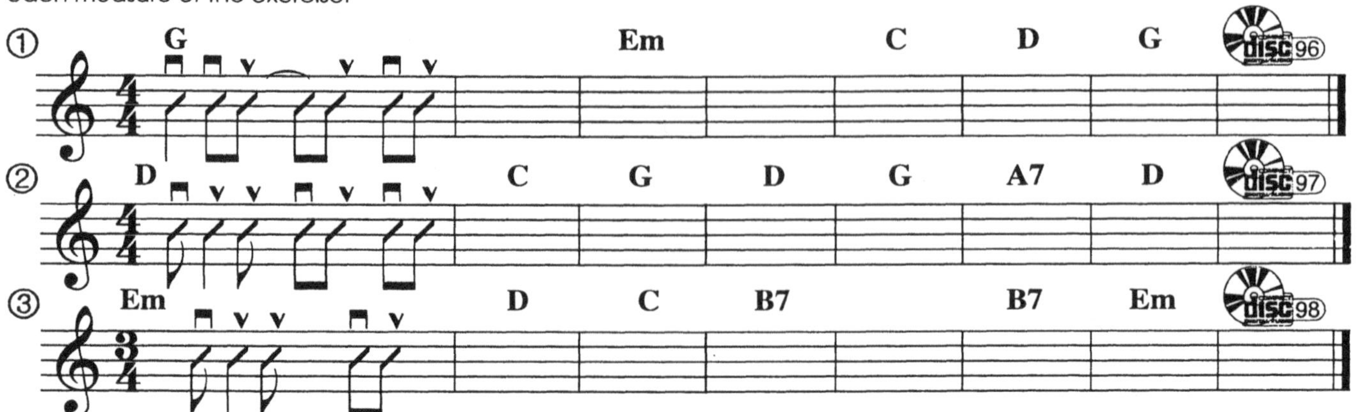